AF265790

SECRET CLASSES & REINTEGRATION

From the Élus Coëns to the
Rectified Scottish Rite

SECRET CLASSES & REINTEGRATION

From the Élus Coëns to the Rectified Scottish Rite

ESSAYS BY RÉMI BOYER AND LIMA DE FREITAS

Foreword by Sylvie Boyer-Camax
Introduction by João de Xango

Rose Circle Publications
Bayonne NJ
2026

CONTENTS

Foreword

to Helle Hartvig de Freitas

The three salutary texts in this book complement and harmonize each other remarkably well. They are offered as avenues of reflection, meditation, and maturation for all those who are willing to listen and hear, to open themselves up to greater and higher meaning. They probably reflect only one aspect of Reality, for who are we here to claim to hold the Truth? But they can say much to those who read with their Heart and let themselves be infused by it. These texts can help them sense the Absolute—the freedom of the Absolute.

Thus, when Lima de Freitas evokes numbers, he specifies: "archetype and number both emerge from the unconscious, in the depths of which **we sense unlimited freedom**."[1] He goes on to say: "This idea **seems to us** immediately *true*. Of course, strictly speaking, it doesn't 'explain' anything, because **everything is a mystery,** but neither does the notion of an *unfolded order*, an *explicit order*, really succeed in explaining anything essential; **at most, it further hides the mystery.** However, the bridge thus built by number between the properties of matter and the ordered processes of our mind, by positing the notion of a 'universal matrix' in which all things are included and present in their totality, from which all things originate, and to which all things return in an uninter-

---

1   Emphasis in bold added.

rupted movement, at least succeeds in making us familiar with the world in which we live and with which we feel a sense of solidarity. **This is exactly the opposite of the feeling of being separated** from universal life by a strange *rational wall*, as is the case with most so-called 'civilized' people,' 'sick from their culture.'"

Thus, it is all a question of looking, of awareness, of attention to what is, of **presence.** St. Catherine of Siena masterfully points out: "Hellfire is the divine light as experienced by those who refuse it." In the same way, Rémi Boyer has been saying and writing for so many years: "All operativity requires inscription in the **'here and now'** so that the **'already and not yet'** can manifest itself."

It is up to each and every one of us to bring forth the eye that sees and the ear that hears, to be attentive to the paths suggested, to the bridges built towards mystery, **to be present to what is,** in order to steer ourselves firmly towards Reintegration and manifest the One.

Sylvie Camax-Boyer

Introduction

Traditional bodies of knowledge can be preserved in two ways: either through secrecy or through total exposure. We have chosen the latter for several decades now. The most internal teachings are brought out into the open. They are thus preserved, available to researchers, and inaccessible to the mundane, who are neither willing nor able to grasp the mysterious link between secrecy and silence.

For many years, we have thus exposed, sometimes in traditional ways, sometimes in new and unexpected ways, what some think to be hidden, others think to hide, but which has always been there for all to see. Without ostentation, many teachings and mysteries have been entrusted to libraries, which remain the richest temples of knowledge, leaving a trail for the *trackers* of the fire of the Free Spirit.

The three contributions gathered here—the first two by Rémi Boyer and the third by Lima de Freitas—seek to question, explore, and traverse the praxis conveyed by the traditions of the Order of the Knight Masons Élus Coëns of the Universe and the Rectified Scottish Rite, two major expressions of the Illuminist current referred to by Robert Amadou as "Martinism," and more broadly of the Western Tradition marked by the seal of Judeo-Christianity.

The first of these three texts deals with an implementation of the theurgy of the Réau-Croix desired by Robert Amadou in the last decade of the second millennium, in response to the state of the initiatory scene in general, considered to be deficient in its capacity for Reconciliation and Reintegration. The realization of this project allowed for a closer assessment of the possibilities offered by the Primordial Cult proposed by Martinez de Pasqually to his followers.

The second text reflects on the essence of the Rectified Scottish Rite or Regime through the central grade of Scottish Master of Saint Andrew, the setting for an exceptional concentration of myths capable of meeting the demands and expectations of the secret class of Professed and Grand Professed, whose real function was never fully established in concrete terms by Jean-Baptiste Willermoz. More than two centuries later, while the Rectified Scottish Rite is flourishing in a world very different from the one in which it was constructed, and while exegeses are multiplying, it seems very necessary to take a look at what this rite preserves, conserves, and offers on the operative level.

The third text is from the pen of Lima de Freitas (1927–1998), a major artist of the second half of the last century,[2] one of the great

---

2   Lima de Freitas, known and recognized as a painter and writer, was also a draftsman, illustrator, engraver, publicist, translator, and essayist. He attended the *Escola Superior de Belas Artes* in Lisbon. This extraordinary man mastered not merely his art, but his *arts*. He illustrated some one hundred books, including the famous *Don Quixote*. His painting has been described as mystical surrealism, but to describe it as such is to restrict and limit it. In 1992, he became a member of UNESCO's Advisory Commission for Transdisciplinarity. He was a founding member of the *Centre International de Recherches et d'Etudes Transdisciplinaires*, in which he worked closely with Gilbert Durand. His works on the 515 of Dante and the Fifth Empire are authoritative. In 1987, he contributed to the *Encyclopédie des Religions* edited by Mircea Eliade. His wife and muse, Helle Hartvig de Freitas, whom we thank here for her unwavering support, played a considerable role in his life as a painter and in his initiatory life, as evidenced by her presence in many of his paintings.

thinkers of Sebastianism, and a high-flying Hermeticist who knew how to seize the arcana in order to realize them. The subject dealt with, Fire and the Number 515, "the Key of Dante," is not specific to the Illuminist movement but permeates the Western Tradition and beyond. This Freemason, Beneficent Knight of the Holy City[3] in the Rectified Scottish Rite of the Grand Priory of Lusitania, then under the wise guidance of José Anes, established himself as a leading Hermeticist and Illuminist master whose teachings reside mainly in his paintings, but also in some powerful writings. "The Fire of Heaven" is a fundamental text, written for Pentecost in 1992, which reinforces and extends the already powerful initial scope of his indispensable work 515, *Le lieu du miroir*.[4] In particular, it takes up many key points identified in his epistolary exchanges with Gilbert Durand. From this "imaginal correspondence" arise revelations of considerable cosmogonic and alchemical significance. Moreover, "The Fire of Heaven" carries many universal initiatory keys that link the traditional teachings we have held over the past twenty years, particularly in the fields of internal alchemy and theurgy, whether these take on the garb of the West or the East.

These texts can be studied, meditated upon, absorbed, grasped, and realized. Five steps towards the Great Real.

João de Xango

---

3   For further information on the Masonic career of Lima de Freitas, see Rémi Boyer, ed., *Correspondance imaginale. Lima de Freitas & Gilbert Durand*, with a preface by Michel Cazenave (La Bégude de Mazenc, Fr.: Arma Artis, 2016).

4   Lima de Freitas, *515, Le lieu de miroir* (Paris: Albin Michel, 1993).

ORDER OF KNIGHT MASONS ÉLUS COËNS OF THE UNIVERSE

An Operative Project
Rather than a New Resurgence[5]

BY RÉMI BOYER

---

5   This contribution is an extension of the foreword to Robert Ho-Than's book, *Pratique opérative des Chevaliers Maçons Élus Coëns de l'Univers*, published in 2017 by the *Centre International de Recherches et d'Etudes Martinistes* (CIREM). It was published in 2022 in the *Bulletin de la Société Martines de Pasqually*, no. 32.

Lima de Freitas

O anjo de shaddai. Acrylic on wood, 1985

to Robert Ambelain
to Robert Amadou
to Jean-Louis Larroque

In the West, there are few so-called initiatory orders that present both a genuine corpus and a set of praxis as coherent as it is demanding. The Order of Knight Masons Élus Coëns of the Universe is one of them, and the publication[7] of the *Green Notebook*, better known as the *Algiers Manuscript*, which constitutes a quasi-mythical piece of this corpus, was a publishing event that brought to a close a series of discoveries spread over several decades—fruit of the tireless work of Robert Amadou.

The turbulent history of this publication is part of the recent history of the Order of Knight Masons Élus Coëns of the Universe, and in particular of the "second resurgence" associated with Robert Amadou. It will be up to historians to write in detail about this episode, adjacent to the history of an inner college that has worked extensively over the last thirty years, in which and for which Robert Amadou played an essential role.

At the beginning of the '90s, my fortunate association with Robert Amadou enabled the inauguration of four projects that had significant development. These were: the creation of the *Centre International de Recherches et d'Etudes Martinistes*[8] and its publication

---

6   Quoted in Simon Leys, *Les idées des autres* (Paris: Plon, 2005).

7   Georges Courts, *Le Grand Manuscrit d'Alger*, 3 vols. (Marseille: Arqa, 2009, 2013, 2017).

8   Officially founded on October 24, 1990 by Robert Amadou and Rémi Boyer.

L'*Esprit des Choses*; the reorganization of an inner college, a vehicle for the three functions of conservatory, laboratory, and oratory; the restoration of an *Ordre Kabbalistique de la Rose-Croix* that would be neither a stooge nor a figurehead, but in line with the wishes expressed by the "Companions of Hierophany" in their day; and the relaunch of the operations of the Knight Masons Élus Coëns of the Universe.

It was in 1992 that Robert Amadou asked me about the Élus Coëns. For him, it was urgent, given the state of the world,[9] to resume the operations of the Élus Coëns. As we saw it, this wasn't a matter of founding a new branch or formally restoring the Order, but of simply getting back to work. The sole purpose of the Order is to practice the ten types of operations. The transmission of grades independently of an operative requirement, on the Masonic model, which has unfortunately been commonplace for the last five decades, ipso facto leads to "apocrypha." What is more, almost all those who speak or write about the Élus Coëns have never practised the said operations.[10] Clearly, they don't know what they're talking about.

The first step was the organization of an informal circle, the *Quatuor Martines de Pasqually*, which brought together a few individuals, members of three or four different Martinist and Martinezist lines, interested in the proposal and already heirs to the first resurgence orchestrated by Robert Ambelain in 1943, in the midst of the world war.

---

9   "The state of the world," wrote Robert Amadou, "seems to justify enlisting in the exasperating battle of Light and Darkness those who are capable of serving." Note from Robert Amadou to Rémi Boyer, dated February 12, 1992.

10 The ten types of operations or cults: cults of expiation; of particular and general grace; against demons; of preservation and conservation; against war; of opposition to the enemies of divine law; to obtain the descent of the divine spirit; of strengthening of faith and perseverance in divine spiritual virtue; for the fixation of the divine conciliating spirit with oneself; and the annual dedication of all operations to the Creator.

The complexity of the matter soon became apparent. We quickly had to distinguish between the letter and the spirit, to give priority to the latter and avoid getting bogged down in overly formal questions.

The question of filiation has been raised. I have insisted elsewhere[11] on the primacy of verticality over historical and temporal filiations. We are prisoners of the linear and rigid Christian calendar, which is in fact a secular form of time that breaks with traditional cyclical times, such as the Jewish calendar. The current overgrowth of the need for historical filiation simply reflects our inability to achieve an axiocracy.

This question of time is essential. All operativity requires installation in the "here and now" so that the "already and not yet" can manifest itself. The meta-framework of our lives is time. Traditional models of time are cyclical or spiral. When we study the implementation of a tradition like that of the Élus Coëns, we need to take this into account to read the figures and to form the operative boards. Too often, we apply a monochronic model of time, based on linear cause-and-effect, when we should be applying a more traditional polychronic model of time (see the work of Edward T. Hall), based on complex equivalences. This view would enable us to "see" and to use ceremony to settle into silence at the moment of the rite itself, that brief part of the ritual in which all is played out, in which the *All* (which, for the Élus Coëns, is also *la Chose*) is played out. We don't operate in time, but in Eternity, which is not a duration, but Now.

Among the Élus Coëns, there are two serious filiations, both apocryphal.[12] The first stems from confusion with the Martinist

---

11　Rémi Boyer, *Freemasonry as a Way of Awakening* (Bayonne, NJ: Rose Circle, 2020).

12　See Robert Amadou, *Martinisme*, 2nd revised and expanded edition (Guérigny, Fr.: CIREM, 1997).

Order and the Grand Profession of the Rectified Scottish Rite (Jean Bricaud – Constant Chevillon – Philippe Encausse and Irénée Séguret – Georges Nicolas). The second was born of confusion in the Grand Priory of the Rectified Scottish Rite, that is, the 1943 resurgence of Georges Lagrèze and Robert Ambelain, in which we find Robert Amadou, Ivan Mosca, and René Chambellant.

In a note,[13] Robert Amadou states:

> When it comes to filiation in particular, we must not give in to Guénonian terrorism (René Guénon has a very peculiar notion of initiation). In the ascertained absence of formal or ritual filiation, the desire of a man or a group of men may join an initiatory society in canonical disrepute, provided that this desire conforms, insofar as knowledge and will allow, to the aim and means of the order to which it is attached.

He adds:

> The success of theurgic works (subject to verification of their authenticity) can provide experimental verification of attachment and, consequently, of the legitimacy of a resurgence.

This was the case for the 1943 resurgence.

In 1992, the Order of Knight Masons Élus Coëns of the Universe was, operatively speaking, dormant. Here and there, Coëns degrees were occasionally conferred, not as ordinations but as Masonic grades, with no operative requirement, by seniority, "equivalence," or for services rendered. Ivan Mosca, in principle Grand Sovereign, had been dormant for several decades. Few were keen to revive a theurgical practice that was as demanding as it was penetrating.

---

13   Note from Robert Amadou to Rémi Boyer, dated February 12, 1992.

We were in an ambiguous situation, at the same time faithful to the 1943 resurgence that had taken place under the extreme conditions imposed by the German occupation, while faced with a totally new opportunity. Indeed, the corpus available to us in 1992 was far greater than that available in 1943. The considerable contribution of the *Fonds Z*, the *Algiers Manuscript*, and other sources made it possible to recast the operative system and scale as closely as possible to the original model. Robert Amadou then noted that, while in form we did not wish to proceed with a new resurgence that would have angered Ivan Mosca, or even Robert Ambelain, in fact, i.e. in operativity, it was indeed a second resurgence that was in the offing.[14]

The *Quatuor Martines de Pasqually* had an ephemeral existence, but nevertheless led to two lasting projects. The first, more pedagogical, was led by Christofer, within the framework of the Temple of Lyon, and is still active.[15] The second, perhaps more experimental, project took the form of the Marie de Gonzague Mother Lodge, which was to open several temples around the world. This lodge and its temples are both still active today. The emergence of these two projects had the effect of awakening a few "sleepyheads." Ivan Mosca wanted to get back to work and take up the abandoned reins. Some Élus Coëns representatives, a little too "masonicized," took a renewed interest in operations.

In coordination with Robert Amadou,[16] the rank of Master-Élu was used as a probationary circle, a place of preparation and observation, a three-year period during which mistakes were still allowed, because the main problem encountered in the operations

---

14 Letter from Robert Amadou to Rémi Boyer, dated September 28, 1992.

15 Having been encouraged by Robert Amadou to place itself under the authority of Ivan Mosca, and then his successor, Phoenix, the Temple of Lyon and other temples born in its wake now form an independent jurisdiction, known as the *Tribunal Souverain de France*.

16 Letter from Robert Amadou to Rémi Boyer, January 20, 1993.

of the Élus Coëns remains that mistakes are forbidden. I remember Gérard Kloppel summing up the situation in a succinct phrase: "With the Coëns, you shoot with live ammunition!" At the end of these three years, by mutual agreement between the Master-Élu and the instructors, it would be decided whether to go further or to leave it at that. This formula proved satisfactory.

Robert Amadou played an essential role in guiding the work in the right direction, being present at every important stage and available to all those who embarked on this spiritual adventure. He insisted on the specificity of the Élus Coëns, on what radically distinguishes it from ancient Rosicrucian Hermeticism, which the term Réau-Croix may evoke, as well as from Martinism, which nonetheless stems from it.[17] In a break with the Coën movement of the first resurgence, he made us understand that the Coën system was above all the vehicle of a cult, the Primordial Cult,[18] and should not be viewed from a Masonic angle, but rather from a priestly one. The grade scale represents not so much an obligatory course, which would have to be followed to obtain Reintegration, as a representation of priestly functions necessary to the operations of the Primordial Cult.

He invited us to consider the cumbersome nature of the Coën system. The system organized by Martinez de Pasqually stems from a very ancient tradition, a current parallel to the Hebrew Kabbalah, which it crosses at certain points but from which it clearly differs at others, and which was aimed at individuals ready to dedicate themselves exclusively to the Primordial Cult, body and soul. The

---

17   This point is developed in Rémi Boyer, *Mask Cloak Silence: Martinism as a Way of Awakening* (Bayonne, NJ: Rose Circle 2021).

18   For a proper understanding of what this appellation covers, it is essential to study the long preface in Robert and Catherine Amadou, *Les leçons de Lyon aux élus coëns. Un cours de martinisme au XVIIIe siècle par Louis-Claude de Saint-Matin, Jean-Jacques Du Roy D'Hauterive, Jean-Baptiste Willermoz*, 1st complete edition published from original manuscripts (Paris: Dervy, 1999).

commitment required is comparable to that of a monk or priest whose entire day is punctuated by the operations of the Élus Coëns, whether minor or major. It is unlikely that, even in Martinez de Pasqually's day, his disciples could apply the system as it was conceived. It was therefore necessary to concentrate on the essential operations and their sequence, which made adequate preparation all the more necessary. Nevertheless, it was decided that every known Coën practice should be experienced for a long enough period to be integrated, even if the practice was not subsequently maintained, as in the case of the four daily prayers. The daily and sustained practice of self-remembering, of silence and emptiness, was insisted upon as an obligation in order to operate. It was also a way of dissolving the identification with the antinomies carried by the Coën system, which appears to be a struggle between good and evil. Any moralizing crystallization[19] can only be disastrous. Operatively, emptiness is essential to bring those serpentine powers in disharmony in the peripheries back to the Center, to install them in a verticality that is both new and original.

Robert Amadou insisted on the necessary precautions to be taken when leading a Coën group:

> In such a lodge, more than in any other, the disadvantages inherent in any human association, even if it is initiatory, must be avoided, and first of all foreseen, with particular acuity.
>
> Ceremonial theurgy cannot be practised with impunity, especially in a form as elevated and powerful as Coën theurgy; know this and take precautions (including the previous point).[20]

---

19 Morals, the fruit of representations of the conditioned person, are necessarily opposed to ethics, which emanate from the Center or Heart, characterized by unconditionality.

20 Note from Robert Amadou to Rémi Boyer, dated February 12, 1992.

It should be remembered that Martines de Pasqually used neither the word "theurgy" nor the word "magic" to designate the practice of Coën operations; it is a "cult," qualified as spiritual or spiritual-divine.

Of course, even though we were able to foresee the obstacles we predicted, we didn't avoid any of them. There were splits among career-minded people, failures due to a superstitious approach to Coën operations, fears, and notable incompatibilities. However, thanks to the group's highly compartmentalized organization, these ups and downs—inherent to group life—never affected a core group of a handful of individuals who successfully carried out all the Coën operations. It took fourteen years for this internal group, based near Orléans, to satisfactorily implement all the operations of the Knight Masons Élus Coëns of the Universe, and fourteen years to form a number of other groups. It was necessary to cross-reference the information on theurgic operations given in the various documents making up the *Fonds* Z with that specific to the *Algiers Manuscript* and other documents, to learn how to use the *Angeliques*, to reduce the uncertainties arising from the contradictions between these documents, to resolve the enigmas posed by practical implementation, and to research and experiment, since only operative implementation is capable of validating or discarding theoretical hypotheses, however perfectly coherent they may appear.

Robert Amadou, to whom every Martinezist, every Martinist and, more broadly, every Freemason owes a great deal, including his detractors, often warned against the premature practice of theurgy, an unpreparedness or misunderstanding of its nature and purpose. Theurgy and alchemy should only be practiced in the zone of silence, outside of concept, outside belief, outside representation. As their etymology suggests, theurgy and alchemy do not address "persons," but "individuals," the indivisible part of ourselves, our original and ultimate reality, the One. The conditioned individual is not concerned with the matter of "Reintegration," any more than with *"la Chose."* In fact, it is the only obstacle—hence our insistence on a pragmatic approach to silence in daily life, reinforced by periods of asceticism to get as close as possible to the axis of pure presence.

The theurgic experience is multi-faceted, ranging from unbridled dualism to nondual subtlety. At first, the practitioner is inclined to think that the celestial hierarchies, the entities with which he associates through invocation, exist outside him. Gradually, he will discover the strange relationship that binds him to these entities, which he nourishes as much as they nourish him. Later, he will understand that the hierarchies exist only within him, that he is their creator. Finally, when he reaches the Center of all things, he will realize that there is none of this. The angel of the turning, as Jean Canteins so aptly calls it, will have done his work to lead the being to Being, within the Real.

This path to the simple, which characterizes initiation, is the one taken by Louis-Claude de Saint-Martin, who, having successfully operated according to the theurgy of the Élus Coëns, internalized it into a cardiac path, i.e. a path to the Center. But let us not forget that you can only give up what you have, only renounce what you've mastered. We'll come back to this point later.

The operations of the Élus Coëns are part of the play of mirrors that unfolds from divine immensity to terrestrial immensity, passing through supercelestial immensity and celestial immensity. This unfolding, the consequence of the two falls in Martinez de Pasqually's system, operates through emanation, emancipation, and creation. Since the second Fall, man is no longer in the Temple, but the Temple is in man, and what is more, God himself has constituted himself as a Temple in the crypt of the world.

The place of the operation seems to be the external, but only seems so, for, working externally, the operator works, through the play of divine mirrors, internally, until he grasps that the one and the many are neither separate nor opposed, that the internal is the external and the external is the internal. Distinction, necessary in the field of creation, becomes coincidence in the field of emancipation, then dissolves through emanation. The two falls are matched by two apparent ascents, but in reality there are only celebrations: celebrations granted to emanated and then emancipated beings, to which the Élus Coëns respond by celebrating the freedom of God even in the opacity of creation and duality.

The game is subtle. It is not elusive for the operator. It is elusive for those who do not operate, since doctrine merely comments on practice. The cult celebrated by the Élus Coëns, this primordial, immediate, and nondual cult, formalized in the duality that is our own, points to the One through multiple reflections which, opaque at first, become clearer until they reach the perfect light of the Divine. While the possibility of a direct path remains, as expressed by Louis-Claude de Saint-Martin after his successful Coëns operations, as evoked by Jean-Baptiste Willermoz and enshrined in the Rectified Scottish Rite, it is less a question of following a path than of celebrating, step by step, in each shade of the divine palette, the totality of the Divine.

The receptions to the various grades of the Order of Knight Masons Élus Coëns of the Universe are not to be approached masonically. They illustrate the operative step-by-step process, and eventually seal it. The step-by-step process itself is carried out by the operations, large and small, of the Élus Coëns. Their function, justification, and meaning are exclusively theurgic.

Of course, it is legitimate to question the effectiveness of the operative system intended for the Élus Coëns. Complex, cumbersome, uncertain… certainly, but it is not a question of efficiency when we celebrate, but of recognizing the beauty and freedom installed here and now through the very fact of celebration. It is because the Coën operative system is understood as a "step-by-step process" that it remains largely misunderstood. It is a "step for," for the step itself, an absolutely free dance within a set of constraints. There is a great paradox in this apparent complexity which, by reversal, leads to simplicity. This paradox is but a reflection of the paradox of God, One and many — One and many to enable the apparent dialogue, the divine monologue between theophanies and epiphanies, between divine manifestations, and the recognition of God by beings in these manifestations.

For more than twenty years, an experimental group, born of Robert Amadou's desire to resume operations, implemented Coëns theurgies, principally the ten or so major operations of Reintegration. These highly complex operations gave rise to reports and evaluations. In any case, access to these reports does not suspend the absolute necessity of studying at length the entire archive of the order founded by Martinez de Pasqually before embarking on this high and demanding theurgy.

Since We Must Operate,
Let's Operate…

A few points with reference to Robert Amadou[21]

Robert Amadou never wished to organize or lead a Coën resurgence, citing "moral incapacity" and "material difficulties."[22] However, not only did he always remain at the disposal of the operative project and the work of the order to which he remained particularly attached ("You have given me great joy in understanding my attachment to the Order of Knight Masons Élus Coëns of the Universe"[23]), but he was its backbone.

On September 28 1992, the day after a meeting of the *Quatuor Martines de Pasqually*, Robert Amadou wrote: "You and I (and Serge[24]) are in complete agreement about not setting up, in an administrative sense, another resurgence (which the group is in a factual sense)." We were looking for the best formula, thinking of isolating the temples from each other, but this could lead to undesirable attachments. In our search for paradoxical and hardly reassuring safeguards, we finally agreed on the substance:

In Robert Amadou's words, "It is necessary, and this is the supreme safeguard, to make room, as much as needed, for the spirit,

---

21 Robert Amadou and Rémi Boyer maintained a considerable correspondence from 1992 to 2004, consisting of several hundred letters, including one hundred regarding the Élus Coëns.

22 Letter from Robert Amadou to Rémi Boyer, March 8, 1992.

23 Ibid.

24 Serge Caillet.

which is in particular the Coën spirit […] There is a specificity of the Coën spirit which brings it, and the corresponding theurgy, closer to the Spirit than other theurgical systems: the religious sense common to our eighteenth-century exemplars made them sensitive to the presence of the Spirit in this spirit" (ibid.).

It was not a question of transmitting Coën forms, but of transmitting the Coën spirit without allowing ourselves to be diverted or diluted by worldly or dual preoccupations. By worldly preoccupations, I mean any form of identification that leads to posturing, which includes the pretensions to hold, understand, and know of all the teachers who feed the quarrels that regularly shake the esoteric scene. We didn't refer to the resurgence of 1942–1943, even though we all belong to it, in order to avoid conflicts, notably with Yvan Mosca. There were no difficulties with Robert Ambelain, not least because Jean-Louis Larroque, a close friend of Ambelain's, also kept an eye on our work. In 1993, Robert Ambelain had approved CIREM's plan to publish the *Algiers Manuscript*, as had Gérard Kloppel.

In a note dated July 1, 1994, Robert Amadou returned to the subject: "Make room for the Spirit! That's how we escape the quarrels of filiation and, more generally, the trap set by initiatory mechanization. About this kind of mechanization, first of all, consider Father Evgraf's little-known yet fundamental criticism: mechanizations run the risk of making us forget the angels. Certain orders, certain societies, certain traditions (I'll say *orders* from now on, for simplicity's sake) go back ritually (mechanically?) to one or two generations before their lawgiver (not to say scene-painter); others claim no more distant human origin; others, finally, who claim a four-century-old patronage (the R[ose]+C[roix]), or three-century-old (M[artinez de]P[asqually], S[aint-]M[artin]), are right to do so if they walk in virtue and power, but the search for physical chains of transmission exhausts and discredits them, both in the eyes of historians (how can we challenge their competence when we place ourselves in their field?) and to initiates, for whom the injunction of the Unknown Philosopher is not a dead letter. 'Spiritual filiation' is the key phrase. But this filiation, which alone counts in the realm of the Spirit (and isn't that the very place of initiation?), and which defines the nature of its means (anti-materialist by definition?), demands uprightness of intention, doctrinal fidelity, and ritual exactitude."

A new lodge, Marie de Gonzague Mother Lodge,[25] was set up to prepare for operations and organize the work, with Robert Amadou's endorsement in order to "avoid the worst from the Coëns Order and disoriented amateurs,"[26] and to respond to the state of the world, as we have already mentioned. The appointment of a Grand Sovereign was ruled out, not least because this project was born of an inner college independent of any partisanship. Additionally, Yvan Mosca, although dormant for many years, could have appeared to some as the legitimate Grand Sovereign.[27]

Robert Amadou invited potential candidates to study five books: *La Magie* by Jean Servier, recently published by the University Press of France, *Les grands textes de la Cabale* by Charles Mopsik, published by Verdier, *Les mystères d'Egypte* by Jamblique, published by Belles Lettres,[28] *La Sagesse des Chaldéens: les oracles chaldaïques*, also published by Belles Lettres,[29] Aryeh Kaplan's *La méditation et*

---

25 The name Marie de Gonzague was chosen for the qualities of this historical figure and for geographical reasons, not for any links with the Order of Knight Masons Élus Coëns of the Universe.

26 Note from Robert Amadou to Rémi Boyer, dated February 12, 1992.

27 Ibid.

28 In English: Emma C. Clarke, John M. Dillon, Jackson P. Hershbell, tr., *Iamblichus: On the Mysteries* (Atlanta: Society of Biblical Literature, 2003).

29 In English: Ruth Majercik, tr., *The Chaldean Oracles: Text, Translation and Commentary* (Westbury, UK: Prometheus Trust, 1989).

la Bible,[30] from Albin Michel, and Alain Ouaknin's *Tsimtsoum*, also published by Albin. He insisted, as he had done previously, on the need to familiarize oneself with Hebrew and its cascades of meaning. He also insisted on the need to practice the "Experiment to convince one of the truth of the central fire axis that is innate in us, without the aid of which no elemental body can subsist or operate," as described by Martinez de Pasqually in the *Treatise on the Reintegration of Beings into their Original Estate, Virtue, and Spiritual Divine Power*. Successful completion of this experience is essential to understanding what creation the operative figures support, and where the operator stands within consciousness-reality.

The importance of page 111 of the the *New Coën Instruction*[31] was at the heart of a number of exchanges initiated by Robert Amadou. Here we find the alchemical tradition. Robert Amadou said, "The idea, which ties in with that of the internal ways, needs to be explored."[32]

Robert Amadou continues: "It would be good for priests, who are theosophists and not just theologians, to question the relationship—which is a commonplace in the Western occult tradition—between 'the body of glory of the internal ways' and the body of the New Adam, the resurrected body. There's a frequent tendency to reduce the liturgical to the operative: yet it is the Eucharist that is not only an example, but the model, the type, the archetype of all transmutation. And the body of the Risen

---

30 In English: Aryeh Kaplan, *Meditation and the Bible* (York Beach, ME.: Weiser, 1988).

31 Fonds Z.

32 The final paragraph of page 111, in English: "Thus do not doubt that it has always been divine word [illegible] even that at all times, the sages have spiritually vegetated and issued from within the matter of iniquity enveloping the soul, as we see also that the reproductive spirit also leaves the earth, stripped of its particular envelope to enter the great universal space in renewal. Now, under the guise of hidden fire, the true seekers of the Philosopher's Stone have inscribed real gold, under the emblem of temporal gold."

que leur enveloppe, car tous savent que ce qui renaît n'est point
ce que l'on avait vû, attendu que c'est Seulement, le Spiritueux
pur et simple qui étant sous la loi de son genre, reproduit son
enveloppe, mais principe Spiritueux que jamais mortel n'a
pu voir et ne peut voir qu'enveloppé, la même chose, nôtre âme
outre son enveloppe corporelle, est encore enveloppée dans l'acte du
peché d'où Dieu l'a rappellée de travailler à Sortir, pour parvenir
à paroître à la fin des Siècles totalement dépouillé, en changeant
en l'homme nouveau, qui n'a jamais connu le peché.

Revenons encore aux sages ci dessus, lesquels, quoiqu'ils fussent
visibles dans ce monde, n'y étaient pas moins, pour cela, éclairés
et echauffés par deux Soleils, à Sçavoir par le divin incréé,
qu'ils Voyaient aussi physiquement des yeux de leur âme que
ce qu'ils voyaient aussi le Soleil créé, des yeux de leurs corps,
ainsi que, S'il plait à Dieu, la Suite de ce traité, de résurrection
des morts, nous le fera voir.

Ainsi ne doutons nullement que cela ç'a toujours été
par le divin Chaleur ceci divin m. que, De tous les Tems, tous les
Sages ont Spirituellement Végété et Sorti du dedans la matière
d'iniquité enveloppe de l'âme, Comme nous voyons aussi que
le Spiritueux réproductif Sort également de la terre, en
Dépouillement de son enveloppe particulière pour entrer
dans le grand espace universel en renouvellement. Voilà
ce que, Sous une apparence de Sens caché, les Vrais
chercheurs de Pierre Philosophale ont écrit du vrai or,
Sous l'emblème de l'or temporel. Mais cet or est purement

One—'firstborn from the dead'—holds the same function with regard to our glorifying practices of the physical body."[33]

There can be no theurgy without the alchemy of the body of glory, or internal alchemy. Jean-Baptiste Willermoz's opposition to Cagliostro and his internal alchemy was mainly due to power plays in esoteric circles of the time, mainly in Lyon. He was well aware that Reintegration requires the alchemy of the body of glory. This is made abundantly clear in the degree of Scottish Master of Saint Andrew of his Rectified Scottish Rite, in which he combines the doctrine of Reintegration with that of the reconstruction of Solomon's Temple, the model for the body of glory. In addition, the drawings of the twenty philosophical tableaux in the *Angéliques*[34] also describe a path to the body of glory. Later, Robert Amadou returned to this question of Angelic tableaux in general. To fully grasp the fundamental, "founding" myth, in its Coën version, "we must," he says, "read the explanation in the figurative drawings (*Angéliques*). These drawings are first and foremost teaching images, and secondarily aids to the drawing of operating boards. Analysis of the drawings in question is difficult, indispensable, and fascinating."[35]

From the outset, Robert Amadou laid down a precise framework, with theoretical papers having practical consequences, such as "*La Chose*" and "*Opérons-donc*,"[36] which were of prime importance in measuring the task and putting it into practice. On several occasions, he insisted that no one should be involved if he had any psychological difficulties.[37] Attraction to what *Belle Epoque* initiates

---

33 Letter from Robert Amadou to Rémi Boyer, dated September 22, 1994.

34 Catherine and Robert Amadou, *Angéliques*, 2 vols. (Guérigny, Fr: CIREM, 2001).

35 Letter from Robert Amadou to Rémi Boyer, dated June 24, 1997.

36 Originally published in *Renaissance Traditionelle*, no. 165–166, January–April 2012, p. 115.

37 Letter from Robert Amadou to Rémi Boyer, dated December 21, 1994.

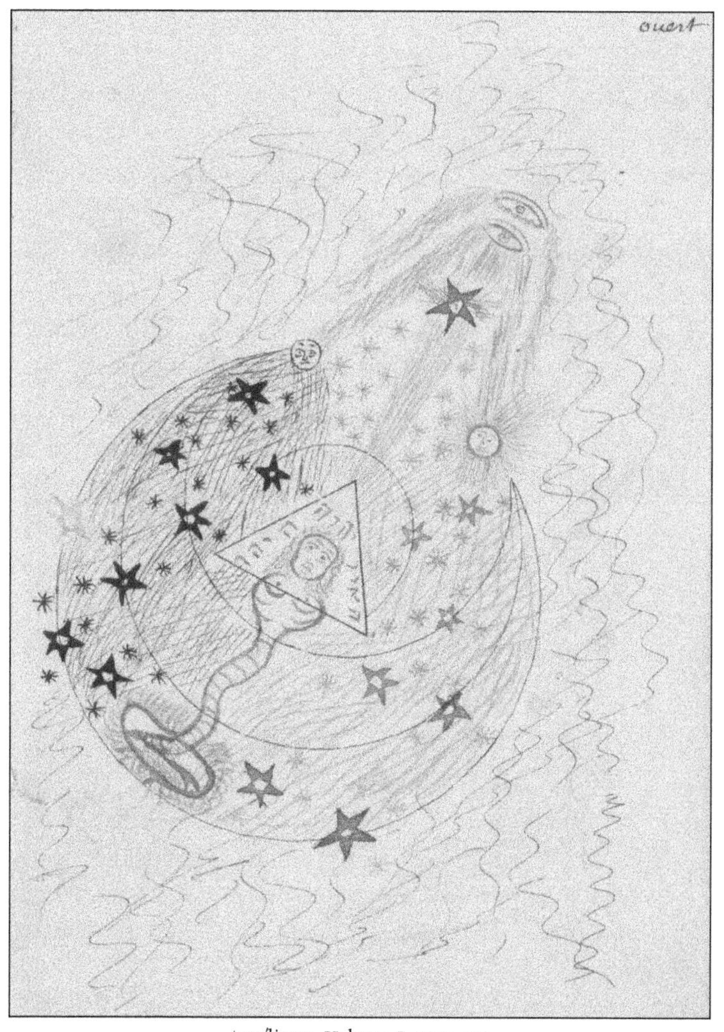

Angéliques, Volume I, page 225

referred to as the "astral" was a criterion for elimination. In fact, the operations of Reintegration have no therapeutic virtue for the person; Reintegration frees from the person. Here, perhaps more than anywhere else, the choice of members of the order and their preparation are key to the success of the operative process.

From 1995 onwards, it became clear that this operative question enabled masks to fall away, separating individuals capable of gathering or acquiring the required qualifications from those simply attracted, sometimes with a certain amount of sincerity, to the representations associated with the Order of Knight Masons Élus Coëns of the Universe, but too little able to make a real commitment. Yvan Mosca revived and wanted to resume his duties. Nothing good came of his initiatives, despite Robert Amadou's efforts to bring the different projects together. Few of the projects favored the operativity that is the very function of the state of the Élu Coën. The Élu is the receptacle of the operation, while the Coën is its being or Being. The operation is the conjunction of two beginnings: "In the beginning, there is the action," the beginning of the Élu, the beginning of the process of Reintegration; "In the beginning, there is the Word," the "beginning" of the Coën who is conjoined with the Spirit. We can understand that this conjunction, installed in reality and embodied by the operation, shatters all mundanities, adhesions, comparisons, and egotistical tensions of all kinds. Only this relationship between the Élu and the Coën establishes the Order.

Most people who wish to become involved in Coën activities quickly give up. The practice of the four daily prayers and those of the equinoxes and solstices are enough to make them realize that other paths would better meet their expectations. On the question of the equinox operations, considered to be of capital importance, it should be remembered that for Martinez de Pasqually, only the Réau-Croix were authorized to carry out the three days of operations, the other brothers and sisters being assigned certain very specific tasks. Some confusion persists as to the date of the equinox operations. According to Martinez's doctrine, but also according to his practice, the date is set according to the Moon, not the full Moon but the new Moon, whether this Moon falls before or after the equinox.[38] In this way, Martinez was able to operate two or three days after the new Moon, working for three days to finish several days before the equinox date. "The Moon governs the forces of increase and decrease," said Bacon de la Chevalerie.

Most Coën operations are too demanding for the uninformed and unprepared. Robert Amadou suggested taking some texts and rites from the *Instruction secrète*[39] to prepare for the operative work. It also seemed to him that the ritual for reconciliation in *Prières et travaux*[40] could be part of a common foundation.[41]

In November 1997, Robert Amadou asked that the question of the Good Companion Spirit be put on the agenda for the December meeting. This was done: "the good companion spirit, which is something quite different from the guardian angel in the banal sense (although it is also a guardian angel), is the Holy Spirit, the Self (not in the Jungian sense), without which there can be no access to *la Chose* and no success in the operations."[42] We see the congruence between *la Chose*, the Good Companion Spirit, and the operation. It is indeed the operative practice, and nothing else, that constitutes the Coën. We approach the philosophies of awakening.

---

38 According to Martinez, exemptions are possible for personal reasons, but also because of the atmospheric situation. Similarly, Martinez considered that there are three equinox months. It is therefore possible to postpone to the next new Moon if conditions are better. Like the waning Moon, the Full Moon is to be avoided, but Martinez also knew how to break the rules if necessary.

39 Fonds Z.

40 Ibid.

41 Letter from Robert Amadou to Rémi Boyer, dated November 19, 1997.

42 Ibid.

Being a "Coën" is a state, the state of the operant, of the priest, the state of the one through whom primordial worship is celebrated in the moment, which is, as we have already said, Eternity. It is not a matter of causality and acquisition, but of free celebration, total spontaneity, beauty, and joy, despite the somber names of these operations. There is a paradox with the Élus Coëns of a dualistic presentation that is hardly reassuring, while what is, what is experienced, is on the contrary nondual and "tranquil" fullness.

Gradually, there took shape a pre-operative program and a progression in doctrinal knowledge,[43] individualized and supervised,[44] along with the indispensable discipline of Silence. The power of Silence is the agreement of *"la Chose."* The framework was tightened; Robert Amadou fearing, above all, deviations.[45] It is the discipline of Silence (which places the "person," that memetic artifice, at the distant periphery of consciousness rather than at the center of adhesions) that was the best indicator of the qualification to operate. The "theocrato-monarchical" approach to the structure of the order, as described by d'Hauterive, had to be transformed into the most rigorous collegiality, leaving no room for personal or organizational prevarication. If the original grade scale was preferred to Robert Ambelain's,[46] in the end, only the scale of operations (most particularly the major operations, one of which appears to be especially central) was determinative.

No one should be fooled into thinking that this has been a

---

43 Thus, the preface to *The Lessons of Lyon* was integrated into the "Welcome Booklet" of the Marie de Gonzague Lodge, with Robert Amadou's consent, supplemented by other texts.

44 Among other things, by the writing of a "physical diary."

45 Letter from Robert Amadou to Rémi Boyer, dated December 5, 1997.

46 At the time of the 1942–1943 resurgence, many documents essential to understanding the system and its operative completeness were missing. It was only Robert Ambelain's great theurgic sense that made it possible to build a coherent system in the absence of these documents, later brought to light by Robert Amadou.

limpid, fluid adventure. We failed to bring together the few Coën groups capable of working together.[47] We were "successful" in our operations, but we can't claim that it was the operations themselves or the internal training required that were the source of efficiency. The "success" of the operations lay not in the physical or semi-physical effects—the famous "passes"—even if certain unexpected phenomena may have manifested themselves, but in the permanently established states of consciousness, corresponding to the various circles of Reintegration. The dreams are significant, when nothing psychological is projected onto the spiritual. Everyone would benefit from deformalizing the interplay of Powers and Consciousness, respectfully stripping away the world of forms to contemplate the absolute structure they reveal. After all, the archangel Raphael is God's healing or restoring power, and doesn't need to be named to work.

The qualifications required to engage and sustain this operative practice are not those expected. Erudition is not necessary, and is even an obstacle. Spiritual instinct is indispensable. In addition to technical qualifications, the qualities most needed are attentiveness rather than "rightness" (let us say nothing about justice; we need to do away with the pretense of knowing what is right), strength rather than "clarity," courage (or better still, the German "*muot*,"[48] a word that is actually untranslatable) rather than "depth," freedom rather than "wisdom." These are necessary if we are to move beyond imitation and be truly creative. The most ancient of rituals is not to be repeated or replicated, but totally re-created. Every operation is a free creation. "*The authentic tradition is not about repeating what others have done, but about rediscovering the spirit that has done these*

---

47 In recent years, only the two expressions born out of the 1992 operative restoration that actually continued the work have come closer together to share their experiences.

48 In Middle High German, "*muot*" evokes both soul and courage, perhaps "fortitude," which the modern German "*mut*" does not.

great things and would do others in other times," said Paul Valéry. The New Man, in the eternity of the moment, operates in Spirit, beyond memories and conditioning, freed from forms. It is in this sense that we should understand the expression "the night of time" as the origin of initiatory traditions. It isn't a question of the distant past, as defined by a dualistic linear temporal vision, but of the axiality of the present moment, of the eternal now, the interval through which an "axial initiatory core" can be actualized.

However, we can only give up what we have mastered, otherwise it is a renunciation, usually dictated by psychological movements and unconscious egoistic tensions. This is particularly true of those who criticized Martinez de Pasqually and his theurgy, the Companions of Hierophany, the Companions of Alexandria, or their followers. Louis-Claude de Saint-Martin was able to abandon the theurgy of the Primordial Cult after achieving success in its major operations. The practice of the Primordial Cult is therefore constitutive of what he was and what became his theosophy. With this in mind, we first sought to operate according to the instructions of Martinez de Pasqually. Once the results were satisfactory, and only then, did we seek to simplify the ceremonial in an attempt to capture the rite as closely as possible.

The tedious research required in the Coën documents, their indispensable cross-referencing, the long and arduous process of setting up prior to the operation, the questions and doubts, are all part and parcel of the operative process. It would be a mistake to deliver a turnkey operating manual enabling the eager Coën to operate without this preliminary phase, which awakens the correspondences within himself and helps to erase the artificial dualistic opposition between internal and external. Once this research has been completed, the grey areas clarified or at least reduced, and the protocols integrated, the work of presence makes it possible to place oneself almost instantaneously in the central operative state.

A tradition from the first centuries of the Christian era has it that Jesus, on the cross, recited the whole of Psalm 21 (or 22, depending on the numbering): "Eloï, Eloï, *lama sabactani*" (in Aramaic: "My God, my God, why have you forsaken me"), or else uttered only the first few words, in effect calling to consciousness the whole of the psalm known to all Jews of the time, just as *"Allons enfants..."* evokes the whole of *La Marseillaise* for a Frenchman. It is this degree of integration of the texts and gestures that must be sought in order to achieve immediacy, the unfolding of the rite then being no more than the celebration of what is already there, fully accomplished. We thus worked according to this triangulation: conservatory – laboratory – oratory.

The Degree of Scottish Master of Saint Andrew: A True Secret Class of the RER?

BY RÉMI BOYER

Fraternal thanks to Fadi Caledit for his comments and questions,
which allowed us to explore the subject in greater depth.

Lima de Freitas
Study for D. Sebastião, mixed media on paper, 1987

"Secret classes" have been a feature of the initiatory world since at least the 17th century. They arise, no doubt quite naturally, from the need felt by a few individuals to share certain qualifications they have acquired, outside of an institutional and organizational framework, beyond the setting of the operative "endpoints" of certain, mostly internal, paths. These traditional classes are sometimes referred to as "internal colleges," or simply "ordo," but can take on all sorts of fluid forms, under multiple names, changing names according to the work being undertaken, or even not being identified by any appellation whatsoever. It is therefore very difficult, historically speaking, to identify them and follow them over time, all the more so as they are generally linked to one generation of seekers in a given stream and die out with the last of them. In fact, we need to make a distinction here between organizations called initiatory (ephemeral, very human creations that wish to extend or replicate themselves over time) and initiatory ways (serpentine, enduring and playing with linear time, appearing and disappearing according to circumstances, favorable or unfavorable).

The sole purpose of secret classes, and the justification for them, is to facilitate the accomplishment of a quest, which remains individual, through free companionship or spiritual friendship. The traditional qualifications sought are commonly those on which

Hermeticism is based and which were taken up by Illuminism: external and internal alchemy, theurgy, magic, traditional medicines, cosmogony, astrology, sacred mathematics, sacred music, sacred linguistics, hermeneutics, the study of mythologies and mythologisms... understood as active components of a process of Reintegration, or recognition, which leads from duality to nonduality, from separation to non-separation, from the many to the One, whatever the traditional and cultural models in which this process is installed, expressed, and carried out, and which in no way concerns the "person," the "self," but rather our divine, indivisible part, our original, ultimate, and permanent nature.

The secret classes raise the question of the deification of the human being[49]: How can I become God? or Christ, the New Man, the New Adam, or Osiris, Apollo, or Dionysus? While the Aristotelian structure of language and cultural biases lead us to pose the question in the masculine gender, the feminine part of God cannot be ignored; she is essential, whether under the name of Sophia, Shekinah, Isis, Artemis, or even Mary or Mary Magdalene. We are in the presence of the unique archetype of the Divine, of a nondual nature, expressed in appearance by a dualistic union between two polarities that never cease to coincide. For those who think such a goal is pretentious or exorbitant, we quote this passage from the Gospels, John 10:34–36, which can be cross-referenced with Psalm 82:6:

---

49   This question is not confined to the classes or to secret societies; it also arises, in a different way, in the so-called profane world, and particularly in the world of science. This is particularly true today with the question of transhumanism and the increasingly blurred distinction between man and machine.

34 Jesus answered them, Is it not written in your law, I said,
Ye are gods?

35 If he called them gods, unto whom the word of God
came, and the scripture cannot be broken;

36 Say ye of him, whom the Father hath sanctified, and
sent into the world, Thou blasphemest; because I said, I
am the Son of God?

The answer to the question of the deification of the human being,
central to the Orthodox Church (while the Roman Church is organized primarily, though not exclusively, around the dualistic question of Good and Evil), is to be found in the ways of immortality,
the ways of Liberation, the ways of the body of Glory, whether this
body is to be created and nourished (the gradualist approach) or to
be revealed in the very moment (the subitistic approach). We speak
of internal alchemies and ways of awakening. The implementation
of these paths does not tolerate large numbers, and secret classes
rarely bring together more than twenty or so individuals.

When Jean-Baptiste Willermoz (1730 – 1824) envisaged the
creation of a secret class of Professed and Grand Professed for a
few chosen Knights Beneficent of the Holy City, he was perhaps
inspired by what was being done in other traditional European
currents, whether Rosicrucian, Hermetic, Egyptian Masonic (the
School of Naples), Pythagorean, or others. In any case, it logically
concluded, from an initiatory point of view, his Rectified Scottish
Rite.

Today, the genesis and rather chaotic development of the secret
class of Professed and Grand Professed are fairly well documented,
thanks in particular to the work of historians of Freemasonry. Let
us just mention three landmarks:

- In 1969, Robert Amadou, under the *nomen* Maharba, published an article in the review *Le Symbolisme*, clarifying the nature, function, and historical origins of the secret class of Professed and Grand Professed. Robert Amadou cleared up many misunderstandings, confusions, errors, and, in some cases, drifting ways of the time. He initiated a rich movement of study, clarification, and analysis that has endured. The article has been republished many times.[50]

- For January–April 2016, *Renaissance Traditionnelle* published a reference issue devoted to the Grand Profession, entitled "La Grande Profession: documents et découvertes, le Fonds Turckheim" with major contributions from Antoine Faivre, Thierry Bourdignon and Jacques Rondat, Paul Paoloni, and Roger Dachez.

- Dominique Vergnolle's *L'épopée des Chevaliers Bienfaisants de la Cité Sainte et de leur Profession*, published by Editions La Tarente in 2021, benefits from the latest discoveries and research on the subject. This indispensable work not only provides an insight into the complex history of the Rectified Scottish Rite, but also offers a better understanding of Jean-Baptiste Willermoz's ambitious initiatory and spiritual project in the pre-revolutionary, revolutionary, and post-revolutionary context of the time.

Jean-Baptiste Willermoz made the RER a conservatory for the Doctrine of Reintegration of the Order of Knight Masons Élus Coëns of the Universe, founded by his master Martinez de Pasqually (1710?–1774). From the Apprentice degree onwards, the doctrine is subtly inscribed in the rituals and their implementation, through symbolism that draws on the two matrices of the Rectified Scot-

---

50   E.g., *Documents martinistes*, 1979.

tish Rite,[51] about which all serious researchers and commentators today agree: the Templarist doctrine[52] and the doctrine of Reintegration. The two referents present in the rite offer (through their increasingly advanced dialogue over the course of the three "blue" degrees of Apprentice, Companion, and Master, and the degree of Scottish Master of Saint Andrew) exceptional material for answering the question of the deification of the human being or the Reintegration of our original and ultimate Source. This creative dialogue finds its pinnacle, its fulfillment, in the fourth degree, which, through symbolism, correspondences, oppositional coincidences, and dynamic orientations, exalts the process of Reintegration or the construction of the Temple of Solomon, which has been the Temple of Man since the "Fall," the "Exile," the plunge into duality that enabled God to constitute Himself as a Temple in the Crypt of the World. Elsewhere, I have outlined many of the elements of this dialogue and many of the avenues to be explored,[53] which I won't go into again here, as that is not the purpose of this contribution. Let us just say that, on his reception, the Rectified Scottish Master of Saint Andrew rebuilds the Temple of Solomon, in particular the Holy of Holies, as a projection and gateway to the Heavenly Jerusalem he is called to join. He is given a jewel, made of a hexagram, which represents (among other things, but powerfully given the context) the path of Reintegration from the doctrine of the Élus

---

51   Caledit Fadi, "Les éléments Coëns dans le Rite Ecossais Rectifié à partir de 1782," in "Le convent de Wilhelmsbad," *Cahier de la Loge de recherche Héritage n°2*, no. 6, GLTSO (May 2022).

52   We call "templarism" that which enables the ever-renewed manifestation of the *Imago Templi*. One of its privileged manifestations is chivalry, as an initiatory function. The Knighthood of the Rectified Scottish Rite and the Knighthood of the Order of Knight Masons Élus Coëns of the Universe provide us with a dual expression of this function.

53   Rémi Boyer, *The Rectified Scottish Rite: From the Doctrine of Reintegration to the Imago Templi*. Forewords by Serge Caillet and José Anes (Bayonne, NJ: Rose Circle, 2023).

Coëns. The hexagram, raised by one dimension, becomes the Merkabah, symbol of the Body of Glory that alone enables us to reach this Heavenly Jerusalem. Several practices of the Body of Glory are potentially inscribed in the symbolism of the grade and the light it sheds on the blue degrees. Let us not forget that the two matrices of the Rectified Scottish Rite, the Solomonic Templarist doctrine and the doctrine of Reintegration, are both part of the great Jewish tradition, and that Martinez de Pasqually was probably a Marrano Jew. His doctrine draws, sometimes unusually, on the immense Jewish cultural and traditional heritage. Recourse to Hebrew,[54] more than suggested by the ritual of reception to the Scottish Master of Saint Andrew, is necessary to identify the operativities conveyed by the myths. This does not mean becoming a Kabbalist, but rather bene-

---

54 *Recourse to Hebrew:* Freemasonry uses Hebraisms, some of them unfortunate. The Rectified Scottish Rite does not. It is the Templarist tradition (one of the two matrices of the Rectified Scottish Rite chosen by Jean-Baptiste Willermoz), the reference to the Temple of Solomon, which leads us by necessity to resort to Hebrew. More than the Hebrew language, it is the extraordinary code of the Hebrew alphabet that interests us, a tool for the grammar of divine creation, in the same way as Sanskrit or Cadmean Greek. This alphabet is considered sacred in Jewish tradition, to the extent that texts written in this alphabet are not burned, but buried or stored until they turn to dust. But the Hebrew alphabet isn't just about the Hebrew language, with its turbulent history. The Aramaic of the Zohar and the Talmud are written in the Hebrew alphabet. Antonio Telmo has described a Lusitanian tradition that applies the Hebrew alphabet to the deeper meaning of the Portuguese language and Latin languages in general. In the 11th century, Rashi (Rabbi Chlomo Its'haqi or Solomon son of Isaac), who left his mark on the history of Judaism, wrote his erudite commentaries in French, but notated in the Hebrew alphabet. Languages written in the Hebrew alphabet have four meanings: the literal meaning, *Peshat;* the allusive meaning, *Remez;* the interpretation, *Derash;* and the secret, hidden, metaphysical, mysterious meaning, *Sod.* In Hebrew, the initials of these four meanings form the word *Pardes* (PRDS: *Pé, Resh, Daleth,* and *Samekh*), the Garden, in which we can access bliss. As each letter is a word composed of letters, there is no end to the depths we can plumb.

fiting from the magnificent cascade of meanings offered by the language itself. Moreover, Jewish philosophy and theosophy, in their multiple facets, do not follow the thesis-antithesis-synthesis schema, but thesis-antithesis-antithesis-antithesis-antithesis... What matters is not what the text means, but what it can say. Isolated, the text means nothing; it is an object within Consciousness, and it is the conscious and unconscious relationship we maintain with it that modifies our model of the world and delivers operative meanings. We are in a state of permanent deepening and permanent celebration. Furthermore, Georges Bernanos taught us that too much analysis prevents us from loving. We must guard against too much profane commentary, however erudite. Historical research, so necessary in the secular world, does not deal with reality, but with discourses on reality. Its methodologies, subject to *Chronos*, in no way enable us to grasp initiation, any more than art. In literature, an author's biography, by focusing on a linear sequence of events, distances us from the work and what it reveals. As Nietzsche warned us, we would like the truth, but all we have are evaluations. So let us look at values. The supreme value of any initiatory process is Freedom. It can guide us "to a higher sense," as Rabelais put it: that sense which the text tells us at a given moment, and which we can freely validate or not for ourselves.

Let us return to Jean-Baptiste Willermoz's secret class project. True Beneficence is Reintegration, to which we will return later. Note: Jesus calls his disciples and fellow travelers "Brothers" only after the Resurrection. Before that, there is only a brotherhood of desire; the true Brotherhood is that of the Heavenly Jerusalem.

The idea of a secret class took shape for Jean-Baptiste Willermoz before the Convent of Wilhelmsbad of 1782.[55] The first article of the

---

55   On the subject of this Convent, considered to be the founding of the Rectified Scottish Rite, we refer the reader to the entire *Cahier de la Loge de recherche Héritage n°2*, no. 6, GLTSO (May 2022).

Statutes indicates its purpose: "The Grand Profession of the Order of the Beneficent Knights of the Holy City is the act by which the Knights, and the brothers of the lower classes of the same Order who are found worthy, are initiated, after the required tests, into the knowledge of the mysteries of ancient and primitive Freemasonry, and are recognized as fit to receive the explanation and final development of the Masonic emblems, symbols, and allegories."

The article tells us little about the Willermozian secret class project. What we do know is that it is not a successor degree to the Order of the Beneficent Knights of the Holy City, since by admitting non-knight brethren, it breaks with the logic of the degree scale. Admission to this class in two degrees, almost two stages of a single degree, gives access to a "final" instruction. This instruction is a synthesis of the doctrine of Reintegration, which has been subjected to a Trinitarian filter. This doctrine is condensed in the *Treatise on the Reintegration of Beings*,[56] whose title as Martinez de Pasqually originally intended was *The Reintegration and Reconciliation of All Spiritual Beings with their First Virtues, Strength, and Power in the Personal Enjoyment that All Beings Will Distinctively Enjoy in the Presence of the Creator*, according to a letter from Martinez de Pasqually to his followers in Paris, dated July 11, 1770. The Treatise was originally reserved for the Réau-Croix, the highest degree of the Order of Knight Masons Élus Coëns of the Universe, the only ones authorized to practice the whole of the "Primordial Cult" through a series of complex theurgical operations. Reading the *Treatise* without knowing the rituals of ordinations and operations, which requires their practice, remains sterile. The instructions for Profession and Grand Profession

---

56   The reference edition remains that of Robert Amadou, Diffusion Rosicrucienne, 1995. On the subject of the different versions of the *Treatise* and the different editions, read Xavier Cuvelier Roy's excellent work at philosophe-inconnu.com/le-traite-sur-la-reintegration-des-etres-des-manuscrits-aux-editions.

are intended to shed light on the whole of the Rectified Scottish Rite and the meaning of Reintegration.

But, unlike other secret classes, Jean-Baptiste Willermoz didn't give very tangible indications as to the means of this Reintegration. For his part, he continued to practice the theurgic operations of the Élus Coëns well into his long earthly life. He envisaged opening the Order of Knight Masons Élus Coëns of the Universe to selected members of the Grand Profession. We also know that he sought other avenues (or perhaps more precisely, other means) which were all disappointments, such as with Haugwitz, Cagliostro (about whom he, along with Louis-Claude de Saint-Martin, was mistaken), the very curious matter of the Unknown Agent, and even animal magnetism. We thus have a sense of incompleteness, reinforced by the failures of the aforementioned secret class and its extensions, legitimate or otherwise, right up to the present day, and yet, more than two centuries later, when we look back at the whole of the Rectified Scottish Rite, its intentions, and its contents, we are also in awe of the coherence of this initiatory architecture irrespective of the stages, negotiations, adjustments, controversies, and events that punctuated its construction.

Robert Amadou (Maharba), in the aforementioned article, writes: "The Grand Profession is not an ordination, just as the Order of the CBCS is not the Order of the Élus Coëns. The theurgy and even the ritual texts are deliberately silent on this subject."

He continues: "The principle points of the secret initiation of the Grand Professed are the nature of initiation and of Freemasonry: a summary of the Martinezist epic in which God, the emanated spirits, the created cosmos, and humanity are articulated, and an interpretation of the symbolism of the Temple of Jerusalem in the light of Martinezism and in relation to Freemasonry."

The priestly function, the theurgic operations of the Élus Coëns, and the chivalric spirituality of the Templars[57] are set aside, but the question of deification remains: How can I become or reveal myself as Christ? How can I reach my true Home, the Heavenly Jerusalem?

Jean-Baptiste Willermoz does not explicitly answer the question, common to all secret classes, of the Ultimate Fulfillment. He may well consider the Coën solution, perhaps out of a sense of ease—it's familiar and almost natural to him—but other answers to the question are inscribed in the rituals of the RER. Any true author, and Jean-Baptiste Willermoz is one, knows that he often says more than he means or thinks he means. It is impossible to know whether Jean-Baptiste Willermoz was truly aware of all that the work to which he dedicated his life brings together, offers, and enables. However, a careful study of the whole of the Rectified Scottish Rite suggests that possible answers to this question can be found in the degree of Scottish Master of Saint Andrew, making this degree the true secret class of the Rectified Scottish Rite. Some may prefer the idea of a class internal to the symbolic degrees, less disruptive to the edifice.

The degree of Scottish Master of Saint Andrew is set in the heart of a treasure box comprising the degrees of the Blue Lodge on the one hand and the Inner Order on the other. It crowns and enhances the blue degrees of Apprentice, Fellow, and Master, and anticipates and prepares for the next class, that of Novice Squire and Beneficent Knight of the Holy City. Its position in the degree scale, its nature, and its symbolic richness make it an exceptional degree, so singular that as early as 1778, Article XIX of the Code ruled out any idea of equivalence with the degrees of other Masonic rites,

---

57　In this respect, the Grand Profession of the RER is totally different from the Professed Knight of the Strict Templar Observance. The former preserves a doctrine, while the latter is in "the Templar remembrance."

and forbade visits by any Brother who had not attained this degree. The initiatory and operative essence of the Regime or Rite is well exposed in this degree, which is indeed more than the mark of the passage from the Old Testament to the New Testament, or from the Old Covenant to the New Covenant. Through its symbolism and doctrinal elements, it reveals the path to the realization of the New Man, the New Christ, the New Adam, the New Hiram. We can read in this degree, in conjunction with those that precede it through a step-by-step rereading, an internal theurgy (Roger Dachez speaks of a paratheurgy),[58] an internal alchemy, specific to the ways of the Body of Glory, which demands to be deciphered. The degree of Scottish Master of Saint Andrew is characterized as "Green," and since the Renaissance, the color green has been used in traditional circles to indicate the presence of a coded language. During the Renaissance, painters, sculptors, and members of the carpenters' and stonemasons' guilds were familiar with a "green language," a visual language designed to deliver secret messages and teachings condemned by the Church of Rome.[59] The call to decryption, a "green" call, which could not be more traditional in the milieu of initiatory societies, particularly Hermetic and Illuminist, is heard in the instructions of the Profession and Grand Profession, certainly, but it is audible at each degree of the RER and finds its full justification in the degree of Scottish Master of Saint Andrew, which places at the seeker's disposal a vast symbolic domain to decrypt and a precise operative path to implement, possibly in an infinite number of styles. A successful hermeneutic frees one from interpretation.

In passing, let us point out that over the past century, and especially in the second half, certain alternative solutions to Coën theur-

---

58   R. Caron, ed., *Esotérisme, gnose & imaginaire symbolique—Mélanges offerts à Antoine Faivre* (Leuvin, Be.: Peeters, 2001), pp. 363–371.

59   Renée Mulcahy, *Renaissance italienne. Les messages cachés des grands maîtres* (Paris, Dervy, 2022).

gy were experimented with. Thus Robert Amadou, who however never ceased to support the practice of the operations of the Élus Coëns,[60] directed some seekers towards the practice of the Anacrise,[61] or in a more simple way, towards the profound art of the Prayer of the Heart—not without success, he confided to us. In another approach, and in the midst of the confusion surrounding the question of the Grand Profession, Robert Ambelain suggested to some of his close friends the practice of the theurgic operations known as "EASIA and EASIE," which in reality belonged to another current, or that of Abramelin the Mage,[62] the only one that worked for him, he further confided. These and other alternative solutions are not, however, born directly out of what the rituals themselves can tell us, especially the so-called "Green" degree of Scottish Master of Saint Andrew.

In the first degree of the RER, the recipient relives the Fall into matter, the heaviest duality. In the Martinezist frame of reference, this is the second Fall. Martinez de Pasqually asserted that ceremonial magic, or theurgy, is necessary because, since the second Fall, we have been incapable of spiritual operations. In a Spinozist way, we might say that we can no longer intervene except at the level of the first kind of knowledge (that of perceptions and forms), or sometimes at the level of the second kind of knowledge (that of causes), but no longer at the level of the third kind of knowledge (that of essences). The question facing us, as we seek to extricate

---

60　On this subject, see the previous chapter, "Order of Knight Masons Élus Coëns of the Universe," and Robert Amadou, "Opérons-donc," *Renaissance Traditionnelle*, no. 165–166, January–April 2012, a text reprinting a communication intended for members of the Order of Knight Masons Élus Coëns of the Universe.

61　Pélagius, *L'anacrise—Pour avoir la communication avec le bon ange gardien*, ed. Robert Amadou (Paris: Cariscript, 1989).

62　*La Magie sacrée ou Le Livre d'Abramelin le Mage*, transcribed, presented and annotated by Robert Ambelain (Paris: Bussière, 1990).

ourselves from dualistic darkness, is: what operativity replaces theurgy within the RER? Beneficence, yes, but what do we mean by that? Societal Beneficence does not require an initiatory order and methodology; it is a spiritual and metaphysical Beneficence that we need to discover and implement in its various forms. The Hebrew word *teshuvah* means to return to one's previous state and evokes reintegration, and its root *shuv* means "good." To "make good" is to reintegrate and be reintegrated, to return to our original and ultimate (in reality permanent) state: "That which remains."

Several Hebrew and Greek words from the Old and New Testaments, with their nuances, are translated into French by the same words, "the darkness(es)" or "the deep." Genesis 1:2 speaks of "a darkness upon the face of the deep." This trilogy of terms is interesting, especially the median word "face." With the second Fall, we lose face-to-face contact with God, turning back to the darkness of matter, risking the destructive deep, the Hebrew *tehom.* The Hebrew words translated as "Fall" in the Bible carry more the meaning of exile than of fall. Note then that historical time, *Chronos,* is eternity in exile.

Man is the recapitulation of creation. Since the second Fall, God has constituted Himself as a Temple within the world, that is, within Man. Darkness is the "external" light, the dualistic light of the world, which, compared to the original and ultimate divine light, is only darkness. Through the principle of the devil,[63] *diabolos,* never so named in the doctrine of Reintegration, the divine separates, in appearance, the One from the many, the uncreated from the created. This is fragmentation and the suffering that accompanies it. The Lernaean Hydra symbolizes this duality, as each severed head gives rise to two new heads.

---

63 It is important to distinguish between the ontological Satan and the separating Satan, the Devil. See Annick de Souzenelle's remarkable work, *Le Seigneur et le Satan* (Paris, Albin Michel, 2016).

Jean-Baptiste Willermoz introduced a dialogue between the two doctrines, the doctrine of Reintegration and the doctrine of the Temple of Solomon, as early as the Apprentice degree. But the fertile interplay of mirrors between the two fully and masterfully develops only at the degree of Scottish Master of Saint Andrew. A double reading, evident (what God gives to see) and interpreted (what God veils) is necessary to discover the praxis inscribed in the mythemes, these compounds of myths.

In this degree, we are indeed offered the path of Reintegration, both in the East and on the chest of the Brethren, by the hexagram pointed in its center, and the reconstruction of the Temple of Solomon, by the ritual. This degree is also the place-state where the quester escapes ternary replication and renews the covenant with the 4, lost since the Fall. Louis-Claude de Saint-Martin explains:[64]

> Explanation of the numbers 4 and 3, which constitute the two natures of man in his present state: the number 4 is attributed to his spiritual soul and the number 3 is that of the principles that make up his corporeal form. The first, giving us 10 by its addition upon itself, presents us with the image of the unity from which it emanates, and thereby announces that its essence is eternal, since it is the same as that of God; the second, not being a unity and having no center, or none of its own, indicates that it is an assemblage that has begun and must end. [...]
>
> Ultimately, the link that binds them together must be broken, and they must continue to drift apart until each is perfectly reintegrated into its source, namely the particular bodies in the general body, the general body in the cen-

---

64 Amadou, *Les Leçons de Lyon*, lesson of Wednesday, March 6, 1776.

tral fire axis, and the spiritual soul[65] of man in his divine principle.

No one can return to the Holy City or Heavenly Jerusalem unless he has rehabilitated or liberated this glorious body, according to the operative approach. This integration is present to the degree of Scottish Master of Saint Andrew in the hexagram, this "new star" that has become "the torch that will guide you on the road," according to the ritual, the double triangle of the East or the Seal of Solomon, which gathers the four symbols of Water, Air, Fire, and Earth into one.

At its center, the letter H represents not only Hiram but Hély, as distinguished from the prophet Elijah, or, according to Martinez de Pasqually, the Rhély, the mysterious figure of Christ, the only indispensable mediator, the spirit of God who animates all the Prophets, including the "historical" Christ, fully, absolutely, Wisdom being the feminine aspect of the Rhély.[66]

---

65 "Impassive soul," says Martinez de Pasqually, which speaks volumes about the state required for awakening, which is anything but passive. It is therefore active, as the Rectified Scottish Rite states with regard to Beneficence, further declaring it to be "universal and consoling."

66 On this point, it would be useful to revisit the typology that runs from Abel to Elijah, indicating the path of the Body of Glory taken by Christ.

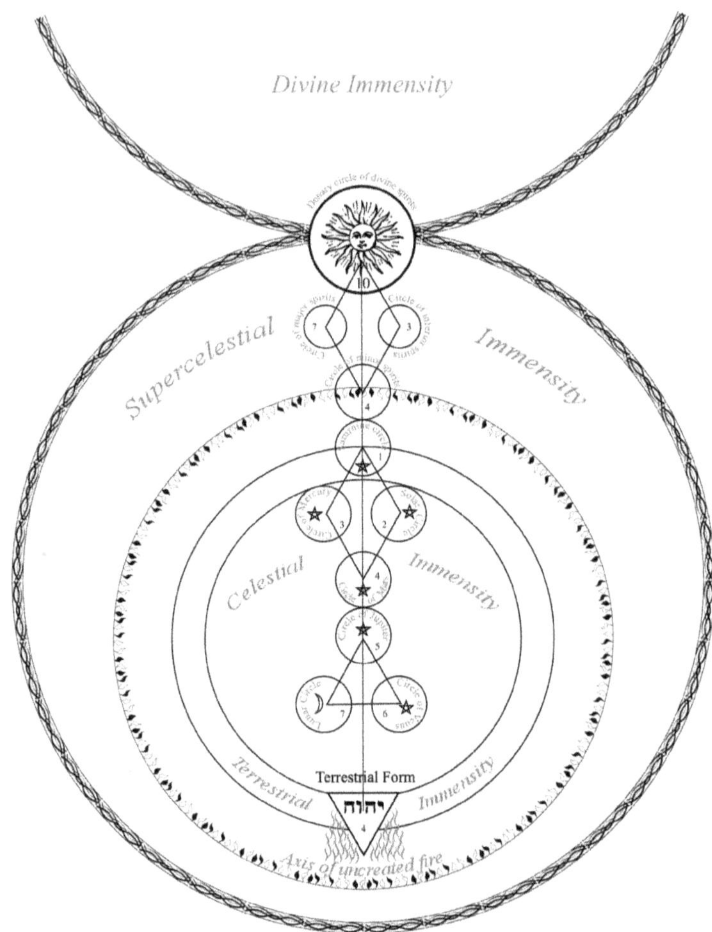

In the symbolic environment offered by the decoration of the degree of Scottish Master of Saint Andrew, we discover another version of Martinez de Pasqually's Universal Figure. We find the seven planets of the Universal Figure in a different arrangement: Saturn in the center (Adam's natural habitat, from which he was excluded during the Second Fall), a Moon – Mercury – Sun triangle, and a Mars – Venus – Jupiter triangle. The observer is on Earth. Facing him are several possible paths to the center, inaccessible without the intervention of Christ or Christ's Holy Spirit, Hély or Rhély.

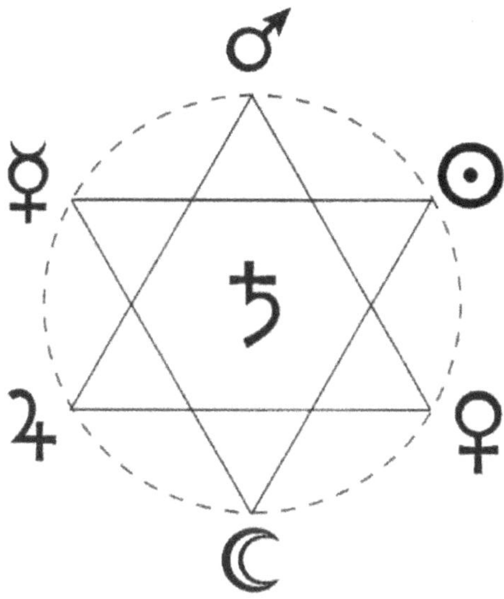

If theurgy (to which Martinez de Pasqually appeals for want of anything better) is discarded, what praxis is Jean-Baptiste Willermoz inviting us to implement? Of course, it is impossible to distinguish between what his conscious intention must be and what stems from the multivalence of the symbols. But let us take a look at what the rituals of the Rectified Scottish Rite can tell us.

We must, I believe, remember three temples of Solomon: the Temple of Stone,[67] the Temple of Paper, and the Temple of Man. In 586 BC, the first of Solomon's temples of stone was destroyed by

---

67   In the second Temple of Stone, there was no golden Ark as in the first. The High Priest had to represent it in spirit. In place of the Ark, there was only a foundation stone. This detail can be seen as an announcement of the dematerialization and progressive spiritualization of the Temple. The dimensions of this foundation stone are (in cubits) $52.3 \times 32.4 \times 32.4$, according to the traditions of the Companionage. We find these dimensions expressed by the Ark of the Covenant in Chartres Cathedral.

Nebuchadnezzar. The Jews were exiled to Babylonia for 70 years, according to Jewish tradition, until the Persians defeated the Babylonians. Liberated, the Jews returned to Judea and rebuilt the Temple.

In 70 AD, Vespasian, then a Roman general, surrounded Jerusalem with his troops. The besieged city was on the brink of defeat when a great rabbi, Yoḥanan Ben Zakai, escaped from the city, reached general Vespasian's encampment, broke in, and greeted him as Emperor. Just as Vespasian was about to punish him, a messenger arrived from Rome, announcing that he had just been named Emperor. Impressed by the rabbi's prescience, Vespasian asked him what he wanted. Instead of asking for an end to the siege and the protection of the Temple of Solomon, Ben Zakaï asked for permission to found a Talmudic school with a few disciples in a small town called Yavné. Vespasian agreed, somewhat surprised by this unexpected request. This event is considered to be the founding of Judaism.[68] This school produced a remarkable body of teaching: Mishna, midrash, Gematria, Zohar, Kabbalah, but also philosophy, wisdom, poetry, Jewish literature, etc. A paper culture succeeded the stone culture. The invisible temple of paper supplants the temple of stone, which will once again be destroyed, heralding an even more elusive temple, the Temple of the Spirit,[69] inner temple, Temple of Man and Temple in Man, to be compared with the primordial cult of the doctrine of Reintegration, prototype of all cults.

This Temple of Man is traditionally made up of four "places"

---

68   Marc-Alain Ouaknin, Philippe Markiewicz, and Mohammed Taleb, *Jérusalem, trois fois sainte* (Paris: Desclée de Brouwer, 2016).

69   And back to the prototype, the *Imago Templi*. Indeed, in Exodus (25:9 and 25:40), Moses is given the opportunity to contemplate the *Imago Templi* and draw inspiration from it: "And look that thou make them after their pattern, which was shown thee on the mount." (Exodus 25:40). It seems, however, that it is sound, more than vision, that is at stake. God speaks to Moses, who cannot see, and dictates his instructions.

corresponding to the structure of Man's spiritual body, as with the "body" of God. It isn't wrong to make a connection, albeit without a piece-by-piece comparison, between these four parts of the Temple and the four immensities of the doctrine of Reintegration: divine immensity (neither dual nor nondual), supercelestial immensity (nondual but containing the intention or potentiality of duality), celestial immensity (nonduality inscribed in duality), and terrestrial immensity (opaque duality). These four places of the Temple, which are also the four "times" *Chronos, Aïon, Kairos,* and Eternity, are the Court of the Women, the *Azarah* (which hosted the sacrifices), the *Ulam,* the sanctuary, and the Holy of Holies. Each of the chambers of the Temple of Solomon can be related to a spiritual organ of the Body of Glory. More generally, the head evokes the Holy of Holies, the trunk corresponds to the sanctuary, the sexual organs to the *Ulam,* with the feet resting on the Court.

Within the Temple of Man,[70] we reach the *Ulam* (abdomen) from the court by the feet (Earth). We enter the sanctuary (ribcage) through the action of the sexual organs and kidneys (Water). We reach the Holy of Holies (skull) through the ear and mouth (Air), the mouth and ear being symbolically equivalent to the female sex. At the top of the skull is access to the Absolute (Fire). Here we have an internal alchemy, analogous in principle to that of Cagliostro and his Egyptian High Masonry.[71] Three alchemical fires are at work: sexual fire, bilious fire, and salivary fire[72] for the total integration by Fire as principle. If, according to Martinez de Pasqually, air is rarefied water, then this process of rarefaction invites us to

---

70 For a more subtle division taking into account the organs of the human body in correspondence with the Temple see Boyer, *The Rectified Scottish Rite,* pp. 64–65.

71 Or more generally to the principle of internal alchemy, whether Eastern or Western.

72 Jesus restored sight to the blind man by mixing his saliva with the dust of the earth and applying this "ointment" to the blind man's eyes.

the death of breath in order to attain this salutary principal Fire. Now, in Hebrew, the letters of the word Ruach, often translated as Breath, *Ruach*, Spirit or Holy Spirit, pronounced slightly differently, *Rewah*, signifies the interval, the access to the divine within duality, the light even within the darkness.

Note that it is from the flesh and not against the flesh that this Temple of the Spirit is built or brought to light. In the second Fall, Adam turns inside out. His interior becomes exterior and *Basar*, his essential flesh, of the nature of the Spirit, is constituted as flesh, an external envelope. There is thus a continuum from flesh to Spirit, flesh being restored to its true nature through the process of Reintegration. The Hebrew expression *Kol Basar* means "all flesh," but also "all soul," and in the Book of Job we read, "In my flesh I shall see *Eloah*," in other words, God.

Another clue may lead us to an internal alchemy. The Lodge, in the RER, meets on the forecourt. The Lodge board reflects the columns, inverted, and the luminaries, the Sun and the Moon. It is a mirror. On the forecourt, the only object that can act as a mirror is the Sea of Brass. It stood in the southeast corner of the inner courtyard (1 Kings 7:39; 2 Chron. 4:10). Jewish tradition tells us that this basin was cast by the bronze-smith Hiram from the mirrors given to the Temple by the women for its manufacture. We thus move from a horizontal mirror in which masks, "persons," egos are reflected, to an ascending mirror that re-establishes the relationship between Earth and Heaven, between "the waters below" and "the waters above." The recipient of the degree of Scottish Master of Saint Andrew will find himself facing this Sea of Brass, a degree in which he is also confronted with another mirror that restores the face-to-face relationship with God. This is the Golden Delta that Master Hiram is said to have worn, discovered by the architect Jabulum during excavations carried out on the site of the Temple for its reconstruction. One side of this delta bears the sacred name, while the other is a mirror.

Let us continue with bronze. According to Isaiah (60:17), bronze is an intermediary between wood and gold, between nature and Light. Another object, Moses' life-giving bronze serpent, is of interest here. The serpent is called *Nechesh* in Hebrew, *Nun, Chet, Shin*, the fish, the barrier, the divine fire. It is the serpent that, at each stage, evaluates the capacity to move on to the next chamber of the body in this verticality which is also a path of Reintegration. Let us observe the relationship between *Nechesh*, the serpent, and *Nechoshet*, the bronze. The bronze serpent of Moses, which destroys the serpents of the Egyptian magi, is a vertical serpent of serpents, redirecting the energy of the serpentine powers that weave horizontal peripheral realities. This evokes the "coiled" energy at the base of the spine, which needs to be given back its upward freedom by orienting it to the "Higher Sense."

This serpentine power, reoriented in verticality, becomes *Yod*, which is also Christ. God extracted from Adam his feminine, Eve, so that he could become aware of her, marry her, and make her fruitful. It is a matter of remembering this part of himself, Eve, identified with the archaic triangle of power – territory – reproduction that sustains the duality of the created, Eve, his *Ishah*, the better to reintegrate her by luminously fertilizing her. In the Here and Now, the *Kairos*, Adam, penetrates the created, Eve, the unfulfilled, transmitting to her the divine seed in the alchemical marriage of mating. He reintegrates *Ishah* into himself to realize divine unity. When Adam turns away from divinity (from his own divinity as well), he impregnates Eve with a toxic, dark substance that disintegrates, crumbles, multiplies duality, and darkens. In *Kairos*, Adam impregnates *Ishah* as Christ, as God. Outside the Here and Now, Adam fertilizes *Ishah* as Satan, the obstacle, even the scandal, "an obstacle that attracts irresistibly." Note that a Hebrew anagram of Adam is Me'od, the quality of the Spirit in man, but also the desire that human beings have for God.[73] Adam's union with Lilith remains incomplete, for Lilith represents pleasure without love. Completion is only possible when Lilith becomes Eve. Adam was the bearer of unconscious amorous incompetence. He becomes conscious of this incompetence through the externalization of Eve. He acquires conscious competence in love by uniting with her. Only by fully integrating her can this competence become unconscious again, fully participating in his completed nature. It is Love that liberates, it is Love that attracts the *Shekinah*, the feminine part of divinity that opens the door to the Heart. Any sanctuary is sacralized only by the presence of the *Shekinah*, which, according to A.D. Grad,[74] manifests itself between the square and the compass.[75] Between the square and the compass, we also find the Ark of the Covenant, the dwelling place of the *Shekinah*. The word *mishkan*, the requested tabernacle, demanded by God of Moses, has the same root as the word *shekinah*. The *Shekinah* can only dwell in the outer Temple if she dwells in the inner Temple, the abode of the Heart.

The Tetragrammaton clearly indicates the transition from ternary to quaternary by the doubling of a letter. IHVH, Iod, Hé, Vav, Hé, features a doubling of the Hé, just as INRI features a doubling of the I. In Hebrew, the four letters I, N, R, I, evoke water or the sea (*Iam*), fire (*Nur*), breath (*Ruach*), and salt of the earth (*Iabeshah*). In alchemy, the ternary *Sulfur – Salt – Mercury* calls up another Mercury.

The ternary IVH — Iod, the Father, Vav, the Son, and Hé, the

---

73 de Souzenelle, *Le Seigneur et le Satan*, pp. 133 – 139. On this subject, we should also turn to the remarkable text, Oskar Władysław de Lubicz Miłosz, *Les Arcanes* (La Bégude de Mazenc, Fr: Arma Artis, reissued 2016).

74 A.D. Grad, *Le meurtre fondamental* (Nice, Fr: Alain Lefeuvre, 1981).

75 For A.D. Grad, from the line determined by the two columns Jakin and Boaz, to the East, is drawn the closed garden, the *gan noul*, "a characteristically female area sealed between the branches of the square and the compass."

Holy Spirit—becomes quaternary by splitting Hé. Leon Bloy once insisted on the intimate link between the Holy Spirit, Lucifer as Light-bearer, the Paraclete, and Woman. Hé splits into two to give birth to the feminine principle, which unites with Iod as the masculine principle. The Hé is the creative energy referred to as the Heavenly Virgin, the Mother of the World, Mary, or even ISIS, whose letters indicate the quaternary serpentine power that implements the creative potential of Iod. This is why Louis Cattiaux tells us: "The holy Name of God is an all-powerful magic in the mouth of him who truly believes and loves."[76]

Another ternary may attract our attention: Hé – Iod – Hé, which is a permutation of one of the seventy-two names of God: Iod – Hé – Hé, inscribed in the Tetragrammaton.[77] This name of God is associated with clairvoyance, but in its permutation Hé – Iod – Hé, it gives us another indication. The first Hé is a window, the second an altar. The Iod is the hand of God, which is why, in calligraphy, every Hebrew letter begins with a Iod, the pure spark of divinity even within duality. Numerically, Hé – Iod – Hé is 5-1-5, 515, the Key of Dante,[78] the number of the *Messo di Dio*, the envoy of God, 515 which we find in the Cross of Saint Andrew, V-I-V. Hiram, as *Abiff*, also qualifies as sent by God. Only one verse in the Bible comes to 515 in gematria: Psalms 21:7, "For the King trusts in the Lord, and by the Benevolence of the Most High he shall not be moved." There is more than a correlation between benevolence and beneficence. They are both part of Reintegration. Only an awakened one, a New Man, a New Christ, a New Hiram, can—and knows how to—do "good." The quester, whether understood as noble adventurer, pilgrim, or knight, is called to

76　Louis Cattiaux, *The Message Rediscovered* (Barcelona: Beya, 2005), XVII: 23.

77　Sebastiano Gulli, *Le Nom de Dieu*, IHVH *dans la kabbale* (Nontron, Fr.: Sesheta, 2022).

78　See de Freitas, *515, le lieu du miroir*, and for an operative synthesis, Sylvie and Rémi Boyer, *Letters to Friends of the Spirit* (Bayonne, NJ: Rose Circle, 2022).

watch. Watching requires guarding. It is not a matter of guarding the Heavenly Jerusalem, which is without adversary, but rather the place towards which it descends, the place of being, which must remain immaculate through the remembering of the Self, the Presence. It is a matter of "keeping oneself close to God."

These few indications, clearly or implicitly inscribed in the rituals of the Rectified Scottish Rite, establish the possibility, undoubtedly infinitely plural, of liberation from dualistic darkness through a conscious reorientation towards the nondual light. If, as Martinez de Pasqually suggests, God begat the Spirit, which begat the soul, which begat the body, the body can be reintegrated into the soul, the soul into the Spirit, and the Spirit into God. This way of Reintegration, the way of the Body of Glory, also evokes the *Merkabah*.

It was Yoḥanan Ben Zakkai, and other rabbis of antiquity, who developed the pre-Kabbalistic tradition of the *Merkabah*, the Hebrew word for "chariot." This tradition is based on the first chapter of Ezekiel in the *Mishna Hagigah*. To cross the darkness of the insurmountable abyss between the soul and the Divine Throne, one needs a chariot, a vehicle of Light, a body of Glory, the *Merkabah*. Now, if the hexagram, which structures the symbol of the degree of Scottish Master of Saint Andrew, like the Martinist pentacle designed by Saint-Martin, is projected from a two-dimensional world into a three-dimensional world, we find ourselves in the presence of the symbol of the vehicle of the *Merkabah*.[79] Operative Companions, especially carpenters,[80] teach that to build the *Merkabah*, you must first master the Platonic solids: the cube, symbol of Earth; the icosahedron and its twenty faces, symbol of water; the octahedron, symbol of air; the tetrahedron and its four faces, symbol of fire; and the twelve-face dodecahedron, symbol of the ether, the Universe, the Whole.[81]

---

79   Additionally, the *Merkabah* is inscribed in a cube. For some operative Companions, the *Cubic Stone* of the Freemasons is a misinterpretation of the *Merkabah* planted in the ground to ensure its stability.

80   The carpenter Companion realizes the drawing from the sphere, then the calculation; from the sphere, he makes an assembly of six crosses. The stonemason Companion draws from the sphere and generates a cube for machining. The roofing or locksmith Companion realizes the drawing from the sphere he then develops and by folding the six points, he assembles and welds it.

81   The tradition of Kepler's polygons associates the tetrahedron with Mars, the cube with Jupiter, the octahedron with Mercury, the dodecahedron with the earth, and the icosahedron with Saturn. In the Kabbalah, the *Merkabah* may be associated with the Sephirah *Daath*, the tetrahedron with *Binah*, the cube with *Geburah*, the octahedron with *Hod*, the dodecahedron with *Yesod*, and the icosahedron with *Malkut*.

Platonic solids (convex regular polyhedra)

 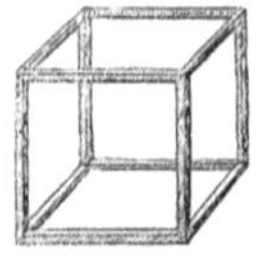 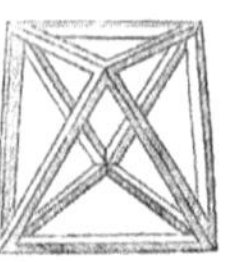  

| Tetrahedron | Hexahedron or Cube | Octahedron | Dodecahedron | Icosahedron |

To make sense within the setting of the Rectified Scottish Rite, our operative Companions also teach us that the dualistic geometry of the line is powerless to assemble certain Platonic solids to make a full volume. It is necessary to apply a "rectification" of four tenths of a unit[82] $(4 - 10 - 1)$ or, symbolically, the quaternary, the denary, and the One. And to assert the adage: "The Orient is worth the line."

When does this turning of the soul towards Spirit begin? As early as the Apprentice degree. A step-by-step look at the rituals of Apprentice, Companion, and Master, in the play of mirrors between our two frames of reference—Solomon Templarist and Martinezist—sheds a singular light on the RER initiation process.

The ternaries are numerous in the Apprentice degree. They carry meaning according to both the Solomonic and Martinezian frames of reference. According to Martinez de Pasqually, the first ternary, at the level of the divine faculties, is *Thought – Will – Action* (or *Speech*) or *Intention – Word – Operation* or even *Thought – Action – Will* (*Operation*). In a Coën catechism, Martinez de Pasqually explains, "The VM designates the thought of the Creator; the Senior Warden, His action; and the Junior Warden, His operation."[83] Note that by taking the middle candle of the candlestick of

---

82 2 x 2 or two tenths for each of the two faces concerned, one for each adjacent volume.

83 "Catechisme de Maître particulier Elu Coën," in Papus, *Martines de Pasqually* (Paris: Chamuel, 1895).

the East, the Venerable Master indicates that it is by the Word that the Lodge is opened.

The ternary is also *Sulfur – Salt – Mercury* in the plane of luminous essences, *Fire – Water – Earth* in the plane of the elements, which correspond to the cardinal directions of *West*, *South* and *North*. The *East* or *Orient* is absent. Is this because we can only contemplate these planes from the East?

The Rectified Scottish Rite takes up a peculiarity of the doctrine of Martinez de Pasqually. We have not four elements but three. Air is considered to be rarefied water. This is not an invention of Martinez de Pasqually; we find this non-Aristotelian ternary in other traditional systems. Water, Earth, and Fire are composed of Mercury, Salt, and Sulfur in different proportions, and according to functions that differ from operative alchemy, Mercury balancing Sulfur and Salt. Salt dominates in Water, Sulfur in Fire, and Mercury in Earth. In the human body, we find Water, Fire, and Earth as well as Salt, Mercury, and Sulfur in varying proportions, according to the organs and parts of the body. Sulfur corresponds to blood, Salt to flesh, and Mercury to bones, but they also correspond to other ternaries: *animal kingdom – vegetable kingdom – mineral kingdom* or *sap – bark – body* or *root – trunk – fruit*.

While remembering that Martinez de Pasqually is not a Trinitarian, but that Jean-Baptiste Willermoz is, let us consider the ternary *Father – Son – Holy Spirit*, which manifests, in God's relationship to man, the ternary *God – Double Power – Good Companion Spirit*, and in man's relationship to God, the ternary *Man – Good Companion Spirit – Major Spirit of Double Power*. This double power is characterized by the number 8, the number of Christ, while the Holy Spirit manifests itself as Spirit, at number 7, in the function of the Good Companion Spirit, the one who leads to Christ. The numbers 7 and 8 are very important in the degree of Scottish Master of Saint Andrew, and are particularly present in the hexagram, whose center is double. Entering the Apprentice degree bent like Jacob under the weight of duality, the Rectified Scottish Master becomes a *Tzadik*, the straightened man, rectified because it is at this degree that the symbols end. In the Holy City, which is not the earthly Jerusalem but the Heavenly Jerusalem, there is no need for symbols. Recovery, Reintegration, takes place especially in the Middle Chamber, the place where, at midday as at midnight, the Master remains on the axis of Presence, unidentified with the peripheries of dual experience. The ascent to the Upper Room begins in the Middle Chamber.

The Sacred Tetragrammaton is, of course, the fundamental quaternary. We have seen that we lost our "face-to-face with God" through the second Fall. The degree of Scottish Master of Saint Andrew aims to re-establish it. This involves a practice enshrined in Psalm 16, which reads: *Shivviti* IHVH *Tamid Lenegdi*, "I have set the Lord always before me." Indeed, not only the sounds of the letters of the Sacred Word, but also their shapes, restore the initial accord with God. IHVH, which is written from right to left, can also be written from top to bottom.[84] The four parts of the Temple of Solomon, like the Temple of Man, or the four immensities of Martinez de Pasqually's Universal Figure, can be found here: Father – Mother – Son – Daughter, or right hemisphere of the brain – left hemisphere – heart – sensorium (touch, smell, taste, hearing, sight), from the Body of Light to the body of skin. IHVH is just as effective in meditation and therapy as it is in the alchemy of the Body of Glory.

However, the turning, the reparation, the ascension, begins at the Apprentice degree. In fact, the lodge is lit by nine lights of order, or Masonic lights: three on the three-branched golden candlestick on the eastern altar, three around the carpet on the southeast,

---

84 Gulli, *Le Nom de Dieu*, pp. 103–131.

southwest, and northwest corners, carried on high candlesticks, and three on the tables of the Wardens and the Secretary. Let us review the lighting of the lights. Before the work begins, the three-branched candlestick must be placed in the room where the Venerable Master and members are preparing. The ritual tells us that it alludes to the "triple power," which orders and governs the world. At the opening of the work, this original triple power comes "from elsewhere," from the Holy of Holies, in fact, despite the destruction of the Temple, i.e. from the divine immensity in the doctrine of Reintegration, to be placed in the East, the super-celestial immensity. The Venerable Master takes hold of the middle candle to light the candles around the carpet, the celestial immensity, from which the Wardens and the Secretary light their own lights, the terrestrial immensity. So it is the persistence of the original triple power despite the Fall, highly sequenced, in the earthly density and duality that is manifested.

Let us proceed to the closing ceremony. The ritual states:

> The Venerable Master extinguishes the three Masonic candles around the carpet, saying: *May the light that has enlightened us in our work not remain exposed to the gaze of the profane.* At the same time, the two Wardens and the Brother Secretary extinguish their own candles.
>
> The Venerable Master then returns to his place, and as he extinguishes the candles of the three-branched candlestick, he says: *My Brothers, when you seek the light you need to perfect your work, remember that it is in the East, and that it is only there can you can find it.*

It is no coincidence that the Wardens and the Secretary each extinguish their candles at exactly the same time as the Venerable Master extinguishes the three torches in succession. The movement of return, of the Reintegration of the divine source, as of the reconstruction of the Temple, is initiated by the rediscovered correlation between the terrestrial immensity and the celestial immensity, and the orientation towards the super-celestial immensity (the East).

Moving from the Middle Chamber to the Upper Chamber requires us to move from the ternary to the quaternary, from the confinement of the 9, 3×3, to the 9 $(1+4$ and $4)$ of the Heavenly Jerusalem, which can be represented either by a square or by two superimposed squares oriented differently at an angle of 45°, thus forming an eight-pointed star.

The 9 is an ambiguous number in Jewish tradition, represented by the circle that both protects and encloses, and a demonic number for the Doctrine of Reintegration since, as 3 multiplied by 3, it gives itself back, indicating the prison of the self[85] which replicates itself *ad infinitum*, leaving no space for our principle. It is associated with matter according to Jean-Baptiste Willermoz, who writes in point 53 of the Instruction of the Grand Professed:

> The number 9 of the third degree designates the assemblage
> of the three ternary mixtures of impalpable elements whose
> union, achieved by a new work of the vital principle that
> is in them, constitutes matter and the material bodies in

---

85   This can be related to the entrance of the Master Mason in chains at his reception of the degree of Scottish Master of Saint Andrew. It is necessary to escape from the captivity of the 9, which implies recognition and knowledge of the quaternary.

the form assigned to each by the Original law that presides over their formation. This number <u>nine</u> designates the end of temporal things because the form of material bodies is preserved only by the presence of this particular and momentary life that sustains their existence for the duration prescribed for each species. For in the universe, everything is life; the smallest grain of sand has its vital principle, without which it would soon cease to exist, and would rejoin the invisible mass of the elements from which it came. This vital principle, as existing separately from the body to which it is united, joins its particular number to the number <u>nine</u> of the material body; it is by this junction alone that the individual exists in its individual form. But as soon as the principle of passive and transient life which held these parts in union is withdrawn, this body remains delivered to its ninth number, which, in the absence of a bond, tends rapidly to decomposition and final dissolution. Then the elements, the principles, and the mixtures of which it was formed return successively to their source.[86]

Ternaries abound in the Apprentice, Companion, and Master rituals. There are three journeys in the rank of Apprentice, five in the rank of Companion, and nine in the rank of Master, which are reduced to three if the recipient listens to the advice of the Wardens. Thus, Jean Baptiste Willermoz indicates how to avoid the 5, which divides the 10, and the 9, which imprisons in the multiplication of the 3 by itself. Through Lodge decorum, he invites us to seek the center of the ternary: the quaternary.

The quaternary, which refers to the Heavenly Jerusalem, naturally evokes the sacred Tetragrammaton, IHVH. It is forbidden to pronounce the Name of God in vain. It is replaced by one of God's

---

86 FM4 507 from the Bibliothèque Nationale de France.

many other names, such as *Adonai*, or *Elohim*, which is plural, or by "the Name." It can also be replaced by the double letter Hé, as we've seen, one masculine, the other feminine, and even triple if we take into account the Hé, absent but present in the Tetragrammaton born of the union of the other two by the *Vav*, a hook.

Every name of God, including the Tetragrammaton, is an approximation designed to point us towards the ineffable. The names of God in Hebrew mark out a unique path for each pilgrim who undertakes the quest for the Name.

It is forbidden to pronounce the Name of God in vain, but it is possible to pronounce it in certain situations. The High Priest of the Temple of Solomon had the power to do so in the secrecy of the Holy of Holies. It is therefore in the highest part of oneself, in the Upper Chamber accessed via the Middle Chamber, i.e. beyond all representation, beyond all identification with the world, beyond all idolatry, in the silence of Being, that the Name can be pronounced. Does pronunciation mean speech? Not necessarily: the Name is present in pure intention before it is enunciated.

We know the process with the letter *Aleph* and revelation. We are dealing with the science and art of the interval. It is in the interval, the Silence, that revelation is received and, at the same time, the commentaries (past, present, and future) of those present and absent. Everything is there, waiting to be actualized. Revelation in Hebrew is *Anoki*, which means "I Am," or a single letter, *Aleph*, which is silent, or is the movement of the larynx just before the sound "A," or that movement rising towards the top of the skull, the Crown, at the highest point of oneself.

In this word, *anoki*, the *Kaph* is essential to grasp the initiatory process.

Kaph means "almost." *Ani* means "I." The word *anoki*, with the addition of *Kaph*, indicates a questioning, a doubt, "almost I."

When Rebecca is pregnant with twins, fathered by Isaac, she is disturbed because the twins are fighting in her womb. We already have an inner duality established in gestation. These twins are Jacob and Esau. They are opposed in everything.

Rebecca, exhausted, finally says to God: "*Lamah zeh anoki,*" "Why am I *almost?*," "Why am I incomplete?," "What am I missing to be fully me?," "What am I missing to be You?" because *Kaph* also means "it's yours." Here, once again, is the question of the deification of the human being.

Esau (*'Esav*) became a hunter, loved by Isaac. The origin of the word is *'asah,* meaning "to make," "to handle," "to manufacture," etc. Esau means "hairy." He was the first to emerge from his mother's womb, with Jacob holding him by the heel. In Genesis, it says: "And the first came out red, all over like an hairy garment; and they called his name Esau" (Gen. 25:25). He is the prototype of the profane, linked only to the archaic triangle of power – territory – reproduction. The word *'esav* means "already finished," while the word Jacob (*ya'aqob*) means "infinite, to be made." Only an object can be finite; a subject not identified with the object, a subject free of all attributes, is infinite. Finitude is a characteristic of the duality, separation, opposition, comparison, hierarchization, lack, jealousy, hatred, etc.— of time!

Esau is described as hairy. Esau is virile, while Jacob, beardless, is more "feminine," androgynous because he overcomes oppositions, making opposites coincide. Christ would long be depicted as androgynous in art before Rome, at the beginning of the second millennium, asked artists to depict him in a more regal form (the model would be Zeus), thus separating out the feminine principle, exalted in representations of Mary (the model would be Isis nursing).

Jacob (*Ya'aqob*) means "he follows" or "he will follow." He is loved by Rebecca. He is the prototype of the initiate who will go from being a bent man (man of desire) to becoming a straightened man

(New Man), a *Tzadik*, taking the name *Israel*. "Jacob" comes from the root *'qb*, meaning "bent," and Israel's root is *yashar*, straight.

We are bent in exile (the myth of the Fall) because we are separated from our true divine nature and are straightened, rectified, by Reintegration. The *Tzadik*, the initiate, is the "green man" or "evergreen man." This is the color of the degree of Scottish Master of Saint Andrew.

Jacob limps, is lame. Lameness is an important mytheme. It indicates dualistic movement, the difficult search for balance, for the center, for nonduality, a difficulty that ultimately requires straightening and rectification. Lameness is observed between two ways, two moments, two breaths, two states, as long as we seek nonduality in duality without finding it.

Jacob's famous dream of a ladder between Heaven and Earth, symbolizing Reintegration, with angels ascending and descending along it, takes place on Mount Moriah, the place where, according to myth, the Temple of Solomon was later built. But the Hebrew word *sulam*, "ladder," also refers to Mount Sinai where the *Torah* ("the Instruction," and in Greek Νόμος / Nómos, "the Law") was given.

The *Tzadik* is "autonomous": he has given himself his own law, freed from contingencies, from the very top of himself, which is indicated by the mytheme of the mountain, which corresponds to the Upper Chamber we access through the Middle Chamber.

Jacob's ladder, according to the *Midrash*, has four levels that evoke the four great parts of the Temple of Solomon or the Temple of Man, or Martinez de Pasqually's Universal Figure with its four immensities, but also the process already mentioned: God begets the Spirit, which begets the soul, which begets the body. By reversal, the body reintegrates the soul, which reintegrates the Spirit, which reintegrates God. The word "reintegrate" can and should be understood in its two senses: "I reintegrate into myself" and "I let myself be reintegrated." This reversal is the key to Reintegration. We must turn away from worldliness or idolatry. In the book of the prophet Obadiah, it is said that "there shall not be any remaining of the house of Esau." The idolaters, those identified with worldliness, caught up in the archaic "power – territory – reproduction" triangle, the real assassins of Hiram, will not survive.

Kaph is a double letter. The ordinary *Kaph* is the bent man and the final *Kaph* is the straightened man, the upright man, the third column, fully re-established, which comes to balance *Jachin* and *Boaz* at the entrance to the Temple of Solomon, passing from the dualistic binary to the ternary.

The two columns *Jachin* and *Boaz* mark the duality of creation, but also point the way to nonduality. The letter *Beth*, the first letter of the column *Boaz*, is also the first letter of the *Berashit* of the Gospel of John, "in the beginning," the beginning of creation or duality. *Beth* means house, and the house creates an interior and an exterior, defining duality. However, the house is home to the couple who seek fusion, union, non-separation, i.e. nonduality. In the house of duality, nonduality is prepared and realized. There are not two columns but three: the third is the human being who passes between the columns, initiable then initiated, bent then straightened (Jacob-Israel). This ternary mirrors the ternary formed by the two Wardens, associated with the two columns *Jachin* and *Boaz*, and the Venerable Master (the East). The two columns are hollow to accommodate the polarized divine energies that descend in spirals and reunite in the human being to return to their source in an ascending modality.

Kaph is the eleventh letter of the alphabet, coming after the visible and opening onto the invisible like the palm of the hand, which corresponds to its spelling. The palm of the hand receives or gives, like a cup. To move from receiving to giving, it turns over, like the soul of the man of desire who ceases to identify with matter to face the spirit.

The oppositional twinning of Jacob and Esau, the initiate and his shadow, which typifies the quest within duality, echoes that of Cain and Abel. Jean-Baptiste Willermoz insisted on substituting the name Phaleg for that of Tubalcain, descendant of Cain, as the password for the Apprentice degree in 1785.[87]

Cain signifies "possession" or "acquisition" and evokes doing and having. Cain is a farmer; he makes the earth bear fruit and depends on *chronos*. He sows, harvests, and plants. He transmits in linear time. He is also a craftsman, builder, metalworker, and blacksmith.

Abel (*Habel*) in Hebrew literally means "evanescent breath" or "mist." It evokes the ephemeral. We think of the Spirit because breath and Spirit are always associated. It is linked to being rather than doing or having, it is fleeting and elusive. It is a nomadic alternative. He is a shepherd, the guardian of an itinerant flock.

Abel is murdered by Cain, blinded by his jealousy. Abel in fact arouses a particular regard from the Eternal One, who seems to ignore Cain. In Hebrew, the word *kina*, jealousy, comes from Cain. Abel dies without a trace and without descendants.

"Where is Abel?" God asks Cain, "What didst thou? the voice of thy brother's bloods, crying out to me from the earth."[88] Note the plural in "the voice of thy brother's bloods," referring to Abel's lost lineage.

To God's question, "Where is Abel?," Cain, in denial, replies,

---

87 Jean-Claude Sitbon, "Trois années après le convent de Wilhelmsbad. La substitution historique du Tubalcaïn par Phaleg dans le Rite Ecossais Rectifié," in *Cahier de la Loge de recherche Héritage n°2*, no.6.

88 Julia E. Smith, tr., *The Holy Bible*, trans. (Hartford: American Publishing, 1876) [a.k.a. "Smith's Literal Translation"], Gen. 4:10.

"Am I my brother's keeper?" It is the only letter Hé that turns the statement into a question.

The opposition between Cain and Abel carries multiple meanings: organization vs. initiation; initiation into the city (Cain built the first city) vs. initiation into the garden; I vs. Self; history vs. essence — dualistic oppositions that we must learn to reduce and overcome.

Solomon was a great possessor (of wealth, power, women, etc.), a man of pleasure, yet he wrote Ecclesiastes, the Insight of Solomon, in which we find the famous phrase "*Havel Havalim Hakhol Havel*," generally translated as "Vanity of vanities, all is vanity." This is a mistranslation; the phrase signifies, "Breath of breaths, all is Breath."

Tubalcain is a direct descendant of Cain. He is the seventh generation, according to the Bible. He is the first blacksmith. Cain built the first city. Tubalcain forged the first sword. Hiram, too, is a metallurgist, a bronze smith in some Jewish traditions, since it was he who founded the Sea of Brass we find in the forecourt of the Temple of Solomon. Hiram and Tubalcain worked with metals, mastering the art of fire. They both know how to work bronze, which is the material of the Jachin and Boaz columns and the Sea of Bronze. But they don't work in the same way. Tubalcain forges horizontally, while Hiram forges vertically.

By discarding the reference to Tubalcain, Jean-Baptiste Willermoz breaks with the principle of temporal lineage. While we can draw up temporal genealogies of Jesus, he is in reality, like Melchizedek, without genealogy, a "Son of God." Jean-Baptiste Willermoz favors the transcendent lineage of Seth, of whom Phaleg is a descendant, a "vertical" lineage, rectifying the absence of Abel's lineage and carrying the possibility of direct access to God, of a timeless filiation, of a Grace, since this is the self-communication of God with himself through the one who makes himself available, like the Master who, in the Middle Chamber, at noon or midnight, on the axis of Presence, is therefore shadowless, once again "Breath" and "Spirit."

There is infinitely more to say. In-depth exploration of what the symbol set and mythemes of the degree of Scottish Master of Saint Andrew can tell us, through either evidence or (on the contrary) cascading revelations, allows us to affirm the fundamental importance of this degree and to present it as the true secret class of the Rectified Scottish Rite, the place-state where Everything is played out.

This is not just a daring proposition. Indeed, it was not until 1809 that Jean-Baptiste Willermoz finally drafted the ritual of Scottish Master of Saint Andrew. He explains this in a letter to Charles de Hesse dated September 10, 1810, from which we quote:

> I announced previously to Your Highness that the almost finished work of writing the fourth degree of Scottish Master had been necessarily suspended in 1789; that the commission which had been in charge of it had given into my hands, once they left off, all that was necessary to complete it, and that this gap in the totality of the general revision had given rise to many requests made from all sides, which I had not been able to satisfy, not daring to take it upon myself alone to complete this work. Twenty years passed in this state; but last year, after the great illness I suffered, seeing only myself remaining of all those who had participated in this work, frightened by the danger I had just gone through and keenly feeling all the unfortunate consequences that would result if this gap in the Rectified Rite were not filled before my death, I dared to undertake to do so. This ritual was published in the reunited lodges of France towards the end of 1809.

Jean-Baptiste Willermoz would not finally rejoin the Eternal Orient until 1824, but by the time he finalized this ritual, he was contemplating his impending death, was then not very optimistic about the future of the RER, and probably knew that his secret class was at best a half-success, more likely a failure. The fourth degree was envisaged as the "hinge" between the symbolic class and the Inner Order. However, it does appear to be the "terminal" of the symbolic class, which is resolutely completed by this final degree, while the Inner Order, to which some individuals, over the history of the rite, will have access without passing through the symbolic class, is of a different nature. We can legitimately assume that Jean-Baptiste Willermoz took particular care in drafting this ritual, to the point of answering the question posed explicitly to the Grand Professed, but in reality already to the Apprentice: How can I ensure my Reintegration, rebuild the Temple, and become another Christ?

Today, although the end of the 18th century is still with us in our time,[89] the conditions of the initiatory quest differ from those of Jean-Baptiste Willermoz's era.

The peripheries of human experience are subject to such acceleration that the risk of "speeding accidents," according to the work of Paul Virilio, is permanent, making it particularly necessary to have the discipline of returning to the center, a place where the forces of dispersion are null. This is why every serious initiatory order constantly insists on the praxis of self-remembering.

This acceleration, which reduces both material and immaterial distances, also allows easy access to traditional bodies of knowledge, thus fostering knowledge and experimentation. (All initiation is experimental.) In the particular case of the Rectified Scottish Rite, we benefit from an exceptional collection of archives and works,

---

89 Philippe Muray, *Le XIXème siècle à travers les âges* (Paris: Gallimard, 1999).

which we can cross-reference with those of other traditional currents, both near and far.

In this new millennium, numerous authors,[90] some well-known, others more anonymous, and several collectives, are making major contributions to our work. Although they do not always agree with each other, sometimes to the point of opposing each other, often for reasons more personal than substantive, or because they forget to distinguish the logical levels in their respective works, all these views on the Rectified Scottish Rite, its sources and contingent manifestations, contribute to its comprehension and influence through the rare mosaic they compose or reveal. If we know how to guard against the inevitable tension between rite and obedience, between initiation and organization, between initiation and personal and collective history, we can turn this traditional repository into formidable material from which to extract one or more initiatory paths, paths of Reintegration that will be revealed at the degree of Scottish Master of Saint Andrew.

Sometimes, when we are faced with the dazzling Light of the East, we need to put our hand up as a visor—to protect ourselves, certainly, but also to see into the distance.

---

90 See, among others: Robert and Catherine Amadou, Emmanuelle Auger, Roland Bermann, Serge Caillet, Dominique Clairembault, Georges Courts, Roger Dachez, Pascal Gambirasio d'Asseux, Thomas Grison, Raymond E.F. Guillaume, André Kervella, Alain Le Kern, Ramón Martí Blanco, Loïc Montanella, Michelle Nahon, Jean-Louis Ricard, Patrick Rodner, Jean-Claude Sitbon, Jean-François Var, Dominique Vergnolle, Jean-Marc Vivenza, etc.

THE FIRE OF HEAVEN[91]

Symmetrical Figures as Symbols of Divinity

BY LIMA DE FREITAS

---

91   This text was published under the aegis of *La Société d'Etudes et de Recherches sur le Cinquième Empire* in the collection *Les Cahiers Lima de Freitas* (Cordes sur Ciel, Fr.: Rafael de Surtis, 2012).

Lima de Freitas
Angel Announcing the 515 to the City

to Helle Hartvig de Freitas

I

Number and Meaning

The God Agni has climbed the peaks of heaven
and by freeing himself from sin
he has freed us from the curse.
—Atharva Veda, 12, 2

The presence of certain Numbers in an uncountable host of legends and mythical stories, sacred or revealed texts, magical systems or metaphysical structures, as well as in the great epics, traditional tales, dreams, and all forms of art, easily convinces us of their fundamental importance as a foundational element carrying meaning, even if this meaning is partially submerged in the unconscious and, therefore, often difficult to grasp. Think of the value always attributed to certain whole numbers, such as the One, always symbolizing unity, of whatever nature it might be, starting with the unity of God; or the Three, as the Evil Triad or the Holy Trinity; or the Four (in which the Pythagoreans saw another aspect of Unity) considered almost universally as the number of manifestation, of Earth, of the directions of terrestrial space, etc. Let us also recall the "mystical" value granted to numbers further removed from unity, such as 12 (for example, the Twelve Apostles), 22 (the number of letters in the Hebrew alphabet), 100 (the hundred Names of God in Islam), 666 (the number of the Beast in Revelation), etc. So many examples assure us that it is no meaningless coincidence that in myths and in certain great religious images we can detect the profound pulse of numbers.

Indeed, number acts as a kind of formal and rhythmic mold which, from the very genesis of myth and in a way that is consubstantial with it, introduces a certain order or principle of clarity into the living and often confused mass of "inspired" narrative, whose dreamlike, visionary nature, rooted in the unconscious, grapples with intense numinous emotions. But in this primordial tension of coming to order, there is no causal procession, number and archetypal image arising phenomenologically together, forming and informing each other in the same movement. Number— or more precisely, the "natural" whole number, the only one "made by God," since "all the others were made by man," as Kronecker put it—participates *ab origine* in archetypal essence. Marie-Louise von Franz, a disciple of Jung who developed the psychological study of number, summed up her thinking on this subject by arguing that number "is the most primitive or 'seminal' manifestation of any archetype or archetypal process. As we see everywhere today processes rather than static structures or orders, I proposed to consider numbers from this angle too: as rhythmic configurations of psychic energy."[92]

A "seminal" manifestation directly from its psychic roots, this means that number is an integral part of *meaning*, of which it constitutes the "atomic," natural, and impersonal core; the added senses, like particles (or planets), form and swirl around it, organized by the affinity of images and words deriving from sensory experience, the memory of these experiences, and the organization of these memories. Number is present from the outset as a rule or structuring principle introducing order into this jumble of instinctive, sensory, and memetic elements, but this intervention is not the imposition of an "abstract" structure purely external to the senses I would call "added," made up of perceptual materials or highly elaborate mental schemas, for already in number itself, as conceived by

---

92 Marie-Louise von Franz, "Quelques réflexions sur la synchronicité," collected in *La synchronicité, l'âme et la science* (La-Varenne-Saint-Hilaire, Fr.: Séveyrat, 1990).

the ancient Chinese for example, there is also a certain degree of concrete "meaning." There is furthermore, correlatively, a certain degree of uncertainty, as in all archetypes: archetype and number both emerge from the unconscious, in the depths of which we sense unlimited freedom. This freedom also exists in number, and is the very space of play. "For the Chinese," writes Marcel Granet, speaking of ancient China, "a rule is nothing more than a model, for their concept of order excludes the idea of law."[93]

This way of looking at number—as well as the correlative notions of order, rhythm, and essential seminal structure—seems much closer to the deep psychological truth, as manifested in dreams, visions, or myths, than the usual notion of a purely quantitative, interchangeable, operational number, an emblem of the formal rigor of scientific "fundamentalism," subject to the oppression of utilitarian logic. Needham, in his work on the ancient science of China, explains that order, as traditionally considered by the wise men of the Middle Kingdom, "consists in the fact that the forms of nature are all meaningfully and spontaneously ordered, like a fabric of myriad reciprocal strands, in the great number matrix of the universe."[94] Marie-Louise von Franz, who carefully studied Taoist thought on this issue, comments: "An esoteric branch of Chinese mathematics concerned itself with this problem by conducting research into the permutations of I Ching hexagrams. Behind this work lies the operation of a cosmic Eros which corresponds to an individual's urge to individuation and which, paradoxically, leads men in the end to a state of universal relatedness with existence."[95]

The notion of *play*, which implies a margin of freedom within

---

93   Marcel Granet, *La pensée chinoise* (Paris, Albin Michel, 1968), pp. 473–474.

94   Marie-Luise von Franz, *Number and Time: Reflections Leading Toward a Unification of Depth Psychology and Physics*, tr. Andrea Dykes (Evanston: Northwestern University, 1974), p. 299, citing Joseph Needham, *Science and civilization in China*, vol. 3 (Cambridge, 1959), p. 163.

95   von Franz, *Number and Time*, p. 299.

the order itself, is not only the elaborate fruit of an old thought in which the seeds already at work in archaic myths have developed harmoniously, it also happens to correspond, quite unexpectedly, to certain very recent concepts in advanced science, such as fractals, where *order* and *chaos* mutually trigger and respond to each other like partners in a cosmic *game* or dance I would call sacred. It would seem that certain archaic intuitions of so-called "primitive" thought, expressed in mythical tales, are finally "corroborated" by the so-called exact sciences, over the abyss of time, civilizations, and languages. One example is the confrontation in Egyptian mythology between the two brothers Osiris and Set, one the god of order and conscious clarity, the other the no-less-divine principle of disorder, chaos, and transgression (which contains the principle of freedom). This confrontation is analogously "recognized" in the work of Mandelbrot, the great mathematician and creator of fractal geometry, where the inseparable concepts of *order* and *chaos* play an essential role.[96] Another parallel: when an unknown ancient philosopher—quoted by Xu Heng (who lived between 1209 and 1281)—asks whether deep knowledge of the arrangements of things in this world will not make us understand "that every thing must have a reason why it is as it is? And also a rule (of co-existence with all other things), to which it cannot but conform,"[97] we wonder whether this is not also what David Bohm means to say. Indeed, this famous physicist, faced with the irreducible contradictions between the basic concepts of relativity and those of quantum theory, has proposed a new notion of order, which he calls the *implicate order*. According to the logic of this notion, "one may say that every-

---

96 Benoit B. Mandelbrot, *The Fractal Geometry of Nature* (San Francisco: W.H. Freeman, 1982). The non-specialist reader may also wish to consult, among others, Fritjof Capra, *The Tao of Physics* (Boulder: Shambhala, 1975); James Gleick, *Chaos* (New York: Viking, 1987); Heinz-Otto Peitgen and Peter H. Richter, *The Beauty of Fractals* (Heidelberg: Springer-Verlag, 1986).

97 Quoted by von Franz, *Number and Time*, p. 163.

thing is enfolded into everything. This contrasts with the *explicate order* now dominant in physics in which things are *unfolded* in the sense that each thing lies only in its own particular region of space (and time) and outside the regions belonging to other things."[98]

We have seen Marie-Louise von Franz evoke a kind of *cosmogonic Eros* at work, it would seem, in the spontaneous arrangement of things, an arrangement "filled with meaning," in what Needham calls "the great numerical matrix" of the universe, and she expresses herself in a sense that applies not only to external things but also to man and his psychic totality, conscious and unconscious. Thus, the "numbers"—or the "gods," for *numen* and *numerus* are very close relatives—at work in natural phenomena, are also and simultaneously at work in the human psyche, which is also immersed ("*enfolded*") like everything else, in the great universal matrix ("*implicate order*") where it finds itself in relation to everything from the atom to the galaxies. Von Franz sums it up as follows: "numbers appear to represent both an attribute of matter and the unconscious foundation of our mental processes."[99] This idea seems to us immediately *true*. Of course, strictly speaking, it doesn't "explain" anything, because everything is a mystery, but neither does the notion of an *unfolded order*, an *explicate* order, really succeed in explaining any-

---

98   David Bohm, *Wholeness and the Implicate Order* (London/New York: Routledge, 1980), p. 225. A little further on (p. 235), the author writes: "Our proposal to start with the implicate order as basic, then, means that what is primary, independently existent, and universal has to be expressed in terms of the implicate order. So we are suggesting that it is the implicate order that is autonomously active while, as indicated earlier, the explicate order flows out of a law of the implicate order, so that it is secondary, derivative, and appropriate only in certain limited contexts. Or, to put it another way, the relationships constituting the fundamental law are between the enfolded structures that interweave and inter-penetrate each other, throughout the whole of space, rather than between the abstracted and separated forms that are manifest to the senses (and to our instruments)."

99   von Franz, *Number and Time*, p. 52.

thing essential—at most, it further hides the mystery. However, the bridge thus built by number between the properties of matter and the ordered processes of our mind, by positing the notion of a "universal matrix" in which all things are included and present in their totality, from which all things originate, and to which all things return in an uninterrupted movement, at least succeeds in making us familiar with the world in which we live and with which we feel a sense of solidarity. This is exactly the opposite of the feeling of being separated from universal life by a strange *rational wall*, as is the case with most so-called "civilized" people, "sick from their culture."

II

Eros, the Hero, and the Five

We shall see that the "cosmogonic Eros" lives on in the most archaic myths, as well as in the articles of faith in advanced religions. In reality, it seems to be deeply linked to what Jungian psychology refers to as the push towards *individuation*, and it particularly manifests itself in the ascending metamorphoses of consciousness. The human being embodies the possibility, introduced into the world, of a more or less limited consciousness, capable of acting on things (as can all living beings, and undoubtedly it is capable of acting on a much greater scale than other living beings), but above all capable of acting on itself. This makes the game increasingly complex. This complexity generally seems to be moving towards total communion with the All in the immobile eternity spoken of by certain mystics, or what "men of light" describe as the knowledge that God, looking at Himself in the mirror of the perfect man, "acquires" of Himself—or that He "will acquire" in the centuries to come, for the created universe, *unfolded*, would perhaps be the movement of this infinite Consciousness in the process of assuming its own infinity, a kind of unimaginable divine "individuation" that has no humanly conceivable end. Numbers would then represent the divine will to know its own abyss; play, the universal dance, freedom, or "chaos," would be the impulses of desire from the abyss, calling and "receiving" this very will.

Eros is linked to the number Five. It is not possible for me to prove, let alone develop, this assertion here, to which I have devoted a number of writings elsewhere.[100] I will confine myself to briefly recalling certain features of this number, anthropomorphic above all others, from a point of view both symbolic (according to the old masters of numerical symbology) and psychological (with Jung and von Franz, but also Resnik,[101] Paneth,[102] and others) as an expansive and transgressive principle, linked to erotic impulses, reversible because it can "rise" or "fall," surpass or annihilate, itself; Five is the number of the "quintessence" or the Philosopher's Stone of the alchemists, i.e., the realized unitary being of the four known elements;[103] for the Chinese it was the "center of the four" and also, as for Western alchemists, the *quinta essentia*, which "represents the most refined, spiritually imaginable unity of the four elements."[104]

Geometrically, the Five manifests itself in the quincunx, or cross, in which these figures are constructed by points marking the angles and center of a rectangle or square; but the fundamental figure of the Five is the pentagon and its pentagrammatic variant. The anthropomorphic projection (in the psychological sense of the word) that makes the pentagon a symbol of man has been a natural association since the earliest times, and derives either from the five extremities of the body, as shown in Leonardo da Vinci's famous

---

100 Lima de Freitas, "515 — A symmetric number in Dante," in *Symmetry 2 — Unifying human understanding*, ed. István Hargittai, Modern Applied Mathematics and Computer Science, vol. 17, no. 4 – 6 (New York: Pergamon, 1989); Lima de Freitas, "Nombres pentagonaux dans l'iconographie égyptienne," in *L'Homme, la science et la nature. Regards transdiciplinaires* (Orléans: Le Mail, 1994); and especially Lima de Freitas, *515, Le lieu du miroir* (Paris: Albin Michel, 1993).

101 Salomon Resnik, "Il corpo, la geometria e l'idea di numero," in *Conoscenza religiosa*, no. 1 / 2 (1979).

102 Ludwig Paneth, *La symbolique des nombres dans l'inconscient*, tr. Henriette de Roguin (Paris: Payot, 1976).

103 See von Franz, *Number and Time*, p. 65.

104 von Franz, *Number and Time*, pp. 120 – 121.

drawing (a man inscribed in a circle, with his hands and feet touching it), or from the digital structure of the hand. For the Pythagoreans, the pentagram was the symbol of man brought to perfection as a "new Adam," in the sense of an ontological completeness and equilibrium that would make him, in the next phase of the *opus alchimicus*, a "divine man" as luminous as a star (like Adam and Eve before the sin, according to rabbinic tradition: not only clothed in a skin of light, but with bodies made of light).[105] This luminous matter or substance of the pentagrammatic star is in reality celestial fire, that is, the purest essence of fire, the "crystal" of a fire transformed into quintessence. Novalis put it unforgettably: "Light is the essence of the igneous phenomenon." And when Dante, in *The Divine Comedy*, writes of God's Envoy that he will be a "Five hundred and fifteen," he is speaking of the same fire that can be said to be "Adamic," of the "second Adam" in whom the presence of God dwells and radiates: God made man, the "Christ," the "anointed one," in whom burns the flame of the bush seen by Moses, or the *Parakletos* who will come, bearing the fire of the Holy Spirit.

The Christian tradition's quest for the Grail is thus a quest for the mysterious vessel filled with celestial fire, capable of nourishing man beyond his desires and transmuting him into a being of light, an emerald Grail containing the Spirit of God. And so, symmetrically, any quest for the *"fire of fire"* becomes a quest for the sacred. The archaic myths of the origin of fire express this quest and transmutation in their language, naive and yet so close to life: either man freely receives the gift of the miraculous igneous substance from heaven, or he transgressively wrests it from the gods; this, in turn, highlights the ambiguity of the Five to which I have already referred and, by the same token, the moral vocation of the metamorphoses—and metaphors—of fire: sometimes divine clarity, sometimes the burning, sooty darkness of the underworld.

---

105 Cf. Armand Abécassis, *La lumière dans la pensée juive* (Paris: Berg, 1988).

For the Sufi, who often perceives a blazing fire, even if it burns only in his subtle vision (*latifa*), this fire takes on the meaning of a symbol of his inner spiritual state, either as the Devil's red, cloudy fire, or as the Sun radiating the light of a divine aurora.[106] The entire *Divine Comedy* is but the Christian epic of the quest for this divine fire, in which the Poet traverses all the ontological and ethical layers of the "igneous phenomenon"—the fire that tortures and punishes the guilty, the fire of repentance that purifies sinners who have become aware of their faults, and the celestial fire of pure light that illuminates sanctified souls.

Let us recall yet another—essential—feature of the rich imagery of fire: the link between fire and speech. In other words, this "isomorphism that remarkably links the summit, fire and speech," as Gilbert Durand so intelligently points out, citing a text from the *Upanishads* in which it says: "*What is the deity of the Zenith? Agni! And what is Agni based on? Speech!*"[107] We find the same isomorphism in the Bible, notably in the founding theophany of the Burning Bush, where the fire that burns and does not consume is seen by Moses at the summit of the sacred mountain, at the same time as he hears the word of Yahweh. The Burning Bush represents the body of man possessed by the fire of the divine Spirit; the Word is the same divine fire felt as a breath that descends through the cosmic axis of Sinai and enters the world of men, where it will be transformed into Law and prophylactic prescriptions. Besides, don't we all know that words can be "cold," "hot," or "fiery," depending on the temperature of the emotional combustions? In its passionate violence, can the word not "set things alight"? And in its ultimate purification, does it not become a word "of light" and radiant silence?

---

106 Cf. Toshihiko Izutsu, "The Theophanic Ego in Sufism," *Sophia Perennis*, vol. 4, no. 1 (Spring 1978).

107 Gilbert Durand, *Les structures anthropologiques de l'imaginaire*, 9th edition (Paris: Bordas, 1982), p. 198.

III

The 515 Mystery

What is born of the flesh is flesh,
and what is born of the Spirit is spirit.
Do not be astonished that I said to you,
'You must be born from above.'
—John 3:6–7

In proposing to subtitle this study "Symmetrical numbers as symbols of divinity," I was thinking, above all, of the famous 515 mentioned in Canto XXXIII of the *Purgatorio*, the second part of the *Divine Comedy*, in which, before a Dante horrified at the vision of the catastrophes that were (already!) befalling Christianity, Beatrice wanted to pour upon the soul of the man who loved her beyond death, the balm of a few words designed to restore the Poet's hope in the saving light at the end of the night. Here Beatrice says:[108]

---

108 See Dante Alighieri, *Œuvres complètes*, tr. André Pézard (Paris: Gallimard, 1965). [English translation: Dante Alighieri, *The Purgatorio*, tr. John Ciardi (New York: New American Library, 1961).] In his commentary on this "five hundred, ten, and five," [French] translator André Pézard writes: "The Apocalypse referred to Nero by the number 666, the total of the numerical value attributed to each of the letters of Nerun Cesar's name. Dante imitates this Hebraic usage, although he at least does not wish to identify any definite character (and the Latin reading DVX is childish). But he compares the hoped-for savior to 'a' Cyrus (as did Isa. 45 ff.) or better still to 'a' Darius, like the one in Daniel 5:31, to an invisible avenger, whatever his name, the one who condemned Balthasar with the obscure sentence *Mene, Tekel, Parsin* (Dan. 5:5, 25). In any case, the number 515 is merely an exemplary allusion and, for the poet, conceals no contemporary or future name. Elsewhere he might as well say, with our old poets, 'un Roland': a common noun" (final note on p. 1357).

> *for certain as my words, my eyes foresee,*
> *already nearing, the unstayable stars*
> *that bring the time in which, by God's decree,*
> *five hundred, ten, and five shall be the sign*
> *of one who comes to hunt down and destroy*
> *the giant and his thievish concubine.*

In the original Italian, Dante writes *Messo di Dio*, "sent by God." So there's no reason to doubt the meaning of this unexpected, seemingly inappropriate and out-of-place number in the Florentine's poem. Indeed, I once asked myself, why designate a God-sent "*cinquecento dieci cinque*"? The answer to this question led me on a fascinating adventure which is described in the book *Le lieu du miroir*.[109] I'm not going to repeat here things that interested readers can read at their leisure. Instead, I'll develop some of the questions arising from my work on the number 515, questions that open up vast new horizons that will no doubt need to be explored in further studies. I will summarize here, very briefly, some of the results of my earlier investigation, so that these new developments can be properly understood.

The mystery of 515 has interested many literary historians and men of letters, attracted by the enigma: from Rodolfo Benini, who suggested, for the 515 transcribed in Roman numerals, the initials DXV, meaning "*Dante Veltro di Cristo*"; to René Guénon, who, while retaining the reading DXV or DVX, rightly refused to see in it Dante's allusion to himself as sent by God, and suggested that we simply read the word Dux—for the Emperor, in the Poet's mind, was quite comparable both to the figure of Chakravarti, the universal monarch of the Hindus, and to the notion of *Khalifat* found in Ibn 'Arabi. Pierre Guérin, for his part, declares the "510 and 5" to be the counterpart of the *Mahdi* of the Arabs or the "Oriental" of Nos-

---

109 de Freitas, 515, *Le lieu du miroir*.

tradamus, and adds that it is a secret of the Ancient and Accepted Scottish Rite; while Kurt Leonhard sees in it an allusion by Dante to Joachimism, coded according to a numerical key that has since become incomprehensible. Dorothy Sayers, for her part, was of the opinion that the precise meaning of 515 has been lost and will probably never be known.

Benini, in any case, deserves the credit of having discovered, by counting the verses that separate the prophecies interspersed in the *Inferno*, that they numbered either 515 or, alternately, 666; the latter number, as we know, is the "number of the Beast" or Antichrist, according to the Apocalypse of John, and also the "number of a man." 515 would therefore probably also be a "number of a man," but opposed to that of the Beast, and therefore a Christ-like number. The use of numerical symbols in Dante, as with St. John the Evangelist, puts us on the right track, since it becomes quite clear that Dante, as André Pézard thinks, was not trying to designate some historical figure, king, prince, or *condottieri* who would come to solve the political problems of the time, but rather wanted to indicate the archetype of the Divine Envoy, half-God / half-man, whose bimillennial paradigm is Christ Jesus. But he would not be the last "*Messo di Dio*" to come to earth, for as we read in John's gospel, Jesus said: "He that loveth me not, keepeth not my words. And the word which you have heard, is not mine; but *the Father's who sent me. These things have I spoken to you, abiding with you. But the Paraclete, the Holy Ghost, whom the Father will send in my name,* he will teach you all things, and bring all things to your mind, whatsoever I shall have said to you." (John 14:24 – 26).

Paraclete means "comforter." His *parousia*, according to the visions of Joachim de Flore, would mark the beginning of the third age of the world, the Millennium, the age of the Holy Spirit. We know what a prodigious impact this Trinitarian conception of history had; its echoes still resonate in our century, as witness Hitler's dream of the Third Reich for *a thousand years*, or the Communist cult of the *new man*, which goes hand in hand with the hope of the advent of a fraternal, classless society. Less well known is the fact that the Calabrian monk's ideas, transformed into an expectation of the Third Kingdom or "Age of Lilies," gave rise to a special cult of the Holy Spirit that still survives in Portugal, despite the traditional hostility of the Church. The paracletic age is still awaited by the inhabitants of the Azores and Penedo, not far from Lisbon, who celebrate it ritually at Pentecost with the crowning of the "Emperor of the World" in the person of a child, the ritual sacrifice of a bull and a collective *agape*, where rich and poor share the same meat and bread. Not long ago, the fire of Pentecost (or of the Holy Spirit) was still commemorated by a procession of lights.[110]

Having said that, let us return to the main question: why did Dante use a numeric sign, 515, to designate the "*Messo di Dio*"? I happened to discover the reason, while verifying along the way the truth of the words of my late friend Raymond Abellio when he declared that in the reciprocal intensification of human consciousness and the vertiginous mystery of divine unity refracted in the archetype of Number, "Numeric Science merges [...] with a spiritual experience."[111]

Two approaches converge in the clarification of 515 as a simultaneously numeric and symbolic structure. The first is based on the geometry of the pentagon, the symbol of the perfect man and *deificatio*, already well known to the Egyptians and adopted by Pythagoras and his followers. A segment joining the first and third

---

110 I have just learned that the festivities of the Holy Spirit, traditionally held in the village of Penedo, near Sintra (a village some thirty kilometers from Lisbon, but rather isolated by the mountainous terrain), which I attended 4 or 5 years ago and which attracted the attention of the general public on the occasion of a television program, have just been suppressed by the new parish priest of Penedo.

111 Raymond Abellio, *La Bible, document chiffré*, vol. 1 (Paris: Gallimard, 1950).

vertices of a regular pentagon forms a triangle that is attributed to the "head" of the pentagonal figure (the pentagon being "upright" and the triangle including the upper vertex): such as Leonardo da Vinci's famous drawing showing a man in a circle, arms and legs spread, marking (with his head) the five vertices of the *pentagon-anthropos*.

This "head" triangle—once called the "luminous delta" by cathedral builders, continuators of the Pythagorean traditions—has interior angles of 108 and 36 degrees; these angles, when seen reflected on the surface of the water, change—a mutation entirely in keeping with Kabbalistic usage—into "impossible" angles of 801° and 63°. The inversion of numbers offers us a key to explaining the symbolic importance of symmetrical numbers, as they remain unchanged whether read from left to right or right to left. Let us not forget that the water-reflecting surface, like the mirror, has a rich symbolic, religious, magical, and metaphysical past, which I cannot go into here, but which strengthens my interpretation of the genesis of 515.

The inversion of the reflected "luminous delta" presents us with a geometric absurdity. For, in fact, the sum of the interior angles of any triangle is always 180°, and here we have the addition of an angle of 801° and two angles of 63°, making a total of 927°! This number is the measure of the "fall."[112] It prefigures the insane—I would say cancerous—proliferation of fragmentary truths that detach themselves from Meaning and fall into the "delirium" of blind reproductions. The archetype of the supreme intellect, the pure

---

112 Note, however, that in the "absurd" figure of 927° we can read the parts 9 and 27, which are respectively the square and the cube of 3, i.e., even in this figure of the fragmentation of divine Light we find, "hidden," the divine trinity "exploded" in space and time. What is more, multiplying the two parts gives us 9 × 27 = 236. Breaking this result down into two parts finally reveals the figure of God's "dispersion" and "sacrificial death": 72. Indeed: 2 × 36 = 72.

number of the angular Trinity bearing the symbolism of divine Fire—simultaneously Light and Heat, Tree of Knowledge and Tree of Life—thus sinks into the "black waters of the Nile" like the body of the slain Osiris. But all is not lost. A grace descended from Heaven may come to bring about a more intense awareness, converting the cursed number of the loss of Sense and restoring the perfect number of the divine Law. This conversion is the gift of the Spirit of God made man, and this restitution constitutes the salvific mission of the *Messo di Dio*. Its number is 515. For dividing 927 by 180 (the *true* number of degrees of the angles of the triangle) gives exactly 515!

The second path to an inner understanding of 515 is rooted in the first vision of Ezekiel, the foundation of the esotericism of the *Merkaba*. It takes place on the banks of the River Chebar—the liquid mirror in which hierophany will be reflected. Listen: "Now it came to pass in the thirtieth year, in the fourth month, in the fifth day of the month, as I was among the captives by the river of Chebar, that the heavens were opened, and I saw visions of God" (Ezek. 1:1). The date provided by the prophet may seem "obscure" from a historical point of view,[113] but it nonetheless provides three fundamental numbers: 3, 4, and 5, the hidden numerical key to the vision. Now, $3-4-5$ refers to the Pythagorean triangle, which we all know from the famous theorem of the same name. The $3-4-5$ triangle is the paradigm of the triangles that verify the Pythagorean theorem. Indeed, the sum of the squares of the legs $(3^2+4^2=25)$ is equal to the square of the hypotenuse $(5^2=25)$. This triangle, too, has a very long history, beginning in Egypt, where it was sacred and symbolized the divine trinity: Osiris the 3, Isis the 4, and Horus the 5—Father, Mother, and Son.

But let us look simultaneously at this celestial triangle and its

---

113 See Moshe Greenberg, "Ezekiel," in *The Encyclopedia of Religion* (New York: MacMillan, 1987).

reflection in the lower waters of the Chebar or, in geometric transcription, inscribe the $3-4-5$ triangle in a circle and trace its "reflection" in the lower empty half of the same circle: behold, we see two triangles united by their hypotenuses. We see that by laterally inverting the "reflected" triangle, we obtain a rectangle with sides 3 and 4, divided by its diameter (which is also the diameter of the circle). Let us say that "Horus" is the diagonal of this rectangle, or the horizon where the upper and lower "waters" divide, or in other words: the place where the two 5 sides of the $3-4-5$ triangles coincide above and below. Note that in the fusion of the hypotenuses $(5+5=1)$ or, in what amounts to the same thing, the diagonal, simultaneously single and double, we already find the 515 nucleus, for unity is "internal" to their union, expressing and summoning it. The force that pushes the celestial Horus towards the terrestrial Horus is the force of *love* (of which the myth of Narcissus is another figure) drawing towards each other their complementarities; the Platonic *sameness* and *difference*, which are but *One* at the beginning as at the end.[114]

In sum, the total configuration of the divine presence in the circle of the theophanic vision of Ezekiel, a manifestation that includes both the heavenly essence and the earthly substance of its "reflection," is thus translated by the sum of the squares of the legs above and below (3^2+4^2), separated by the common hypotenuse $(5+5=1)$ whose square is 1. So we have $25-1-25$. Extracting the square roots yields the *Messo di Dio* number: $5-1-5$.

---

114 The great Sufi Jalāl al-Dīn Rūmī declares in a well-known quatrain:
    Between us the Thou and the I have ceased.
    I am not I, Thou art not Thou, nor art Thou I.
    I am at once I and Thou, Thou art at once Thou and I.
    —Ernst Cassirer, *The Philosophy of Symbolic Forms*, vol. 2 "Mythical Thought" (New Haven: Yale University, 1955), p. 231.

IV

The Number of Celestial Fire

Brahma is identical to fire.
—Bhagavad Gita, 4:25

Having explained—too quickly!—the mystery of 515, I'll move on to the *Celestial Fire* aspect of this same Number, in other words, to the study of 515 as the number of the fire of heaven. We've already touched on this aspect by mentioning the fire of Pentecost (the flames descending on the heads of the apostles) or the Fire of the Holy Spirit. But we need to go a step further and see how this fire from heaven, either embodied in civilizing heroes or deities descended to earth (such as the *Messo di Dio* or the Christic figure of the Son), or manifested in the sensible world as power or acting force, constitutes the essential principle of the Five and the Pentagon. For the Hindus, there are five fires "incarnated" in the deities: an earthly fire (*Agni*); an intermediary fire of lightning (*Indra*); a celestial fire, essentially solar (*Surya*); and two other types of fire, that of "penetration" or "absorption" (*Vaishvanara*), and that of destruction, which is another aspect of Agni; there are also, in parallel, *five* aspects of ritual fire. We have also seen that the hypotenuse of the Pythagorean triangle manifests the Five, which is the "number of a man." I would like now to draw some unexpected conclusions for the study of iconography and myth, and cite a few illuminating examples from among the many crystallizations of symbol and myth that relate directly to the numbers and symmetries of the pentagon.

Indeed, the symmetrical structure of 515, which I believe stems from a secret tradition with Egyptian roots (known to the Knights Templar, but which Dante was the first — and the last, as far as I know — to make literary use of as a prophetic symbol), postulates the hypostatic union of human nature and divine essence: the first is expressed by the 5–5 polarization, which morphologically derives, of course, from the opposition of the two hands, or more precisely the 5 fingers of each hand, right and left, "masculine" and "feminine"; and the second, the divine essence, is revealed by the axial and medial 1, "hidden" like a spine at the center and inside the digital duality. It is as if the joining of the two hands — an ancestral gesture of prayer — by bringing two complementary "fires" into contact provokes the blossoming of something entirely different, a "Son," in which Divine Fire manifests itself as the reconquered unity and renewed power of life. The joining of hands thus becomes an act of love from which bursts forth a flame that is absolutely life-creating and therefore essentially divine.

We need to distinguish between two fires: there is the banal, "technical" fire (but even this often seems to retain traces of the principal igneous core from which phenomenal manifestations derive), and there is the other, the principal, "celestial" fire (the equivalent of the secret fire of the alchemists, and also of the fire of divine love "that burns unseen" sung by Camões); the magic of the shaman, "the lord of fire," which enables him to touch a red-hot iron, to walk on embers with impunity, or to provoke a very strong heat inside his body, proves that he can submit ordinary fire to his will, and that there exists a purer and more powerful fire, of spiritual essence.

But if the Divine Fire is symbolized by the Triangle (either equilateral in its abstract, principal, and transcendent perfection, or "Pythagorean" — the 3–4–5 triangle — in the visible manifestation of His Face, as in the first vision of Ezekiel), as soon as it becomes Man and terrestrial life, it becomes the double Five, thus inaugurating the indefinite series of pentagonal avatars of life, death, and resurrection. Indeed, for the ancient Egyptians and Pythagoreans alike, 5 is the anthropomorphic number *par excellence*. The regular pentagon is the symbol of the Perfect Man, and the pentagram or star pentagon is the *signatura* of the *deificatio* or Immortal Man, "the most powerful sign of all," according to Paracelsus. The pentagram produces cascades of irrational numbers and radiates spiral pulsations. There is certainly an energy in the number five and its geometric figures that is somehow *exorbitant*, transgressive, ardent, and erotic in its most direct manifestations, deriving from its igneous nature. Bachelard studied the ambiguous nature of man's idea of fire through a kind of psychoanalysis of alchemical and poetic texts, which refer to a "sexualized fire"; less an analyst and closer to the symbol than the epiphenomenon, I prefer to think of fire as *sexualizing*. It might be necessary to reprise the entire chapter of my book *Le lieu du miroir* dedicated to the most active dynamisms of the Pentad; I'll confine myself to retracing, along a different path, the process of the appearance of the *star* within the pentagon:

> From a cosmogenetic point of view, the perfect equilateral Triangle, in its absolutely balanced tri-unity, must "contract" to leave "room" for manifestation, which causes the Spirit of God to "locate" itself above the waters, thus creating a shimmer where the pre-image of man in his pentagonal polarization is already taking shape, containing the promise of the more complex unity formed by $5 + 5$ (and we will thus have traversed the entire path from Unity-in-itself, 1, to 10, or the One-manifested-for-itself).
>
> But from the point of view of Anthropogenesis, we could summarize the formative process, from the Celestial Fire that created man to the Divinized or Celestial Man, in

five essential steps: first, the junction of Divine Breath and Earth, which were, before the beginning, Divine Fire above the waters and empty Earth no more than the support of forms; this junction is still no more than a simple addition $(3+4)$ in which each archetypal pre-form retains its own center; yet it is already a human figure, if you like, for the bonding of triangle and square heralds the disappearance of the "membrane" of contact, at the same time as the number of sides has dropped from 7 to 6 (5 outside and one inside the figure, where the base of the triangle and the upper side of the square merge); soon there will be just 5 sides, through the elimination of the inner boundary. For this to happen, a "loving" impulse must push the poles of consciousness of the 3 and the 4 towards each other (grace descending, faith ascending); this already (imperfectly) pentagonal shape, within which a "fire" of love moves the two "hearts" towards union, corresponds to the alchemists' "marriage of Fire and Earth": Earth is "dissolved" and then "sublimated"; if we then "clip the wings of the spirit," if we "sublimate," we will have a "pure salt," the "salt of the 'earthly mix,'" and we will have completed the marriage of earth and heaven.[115] This figure is a geometric symbol of the "Philosopher's Stone" or Athanor. It burns. The result of this "coction" will be something entirely new: the pentagon, a figure with a single center, from which emanates a "wave of order" that soon equalizes the interior angles and triggers the second internal "coction." Indeed, the dynamisms generated by this new form of unified consciousness (stabilized consciousness of the four in the form of the five, power of the consciousness of consciousness, or "center of the four") are so

---

115 See the chapter "Sexualized Fire" in Gaston Bachelard, *The Psychoanalysis of Fire*, tr. Alan C. M. Ross (Boston: Beacon Press, 1964), pp. 43–58.

energetic that polarized tensions jump like electric sparks
from pole to pole, vertex to vertex. This will give rise, once
again, to a new, entirely different figure, the pentagram or
star pentagon. This is the second "Philosopher's Stone," this
time truly "in the red" as the Fire of Heaven shines through
it like a star in the firmament. (Has anyone noticed that, for
the Egyptians, the stars are always pentagonal?)

Of course, many dangers lurk around such metamorphoses. In any
case, it is significant that the vertices of the pentagon, starred or
not, because they are five, always pose the problem of an unsuc-
cessful coupling, to use the language of the sexualization of fire;
there will always be a solitary pole, without a peer, "exiled" outside the "square"— or coupling with a pole already taken, and thus
transgressive, regressive (because we are back to the triangle!), and
therefore guilty; in other words, there will always be a fifth outcast,
a source of rebellion, fermenting change, whether destructive, in-
novative, or even creative. Man, like the fallen angel, trembles with
dissatisfaction and impatience, and like the pentagon, he is ready to
explode. For from the pentagon can spring inexhaustible torrents
of golden numbers, in the vertigo of logarithmic growth—or
decline—in the excess and inflation that constantly threaten.

The paradigm of the "Son" or the Five, the "amphibian" of
Heaven and Earth, the Christ, by expiring on the cross, teaches us
that the value of sacrifice (a word which means "to make sacred")
derives from the Son's acceptance of the Son's exclusion, thus becoming the Unique, whose Bride is the Cross, in other words, the
stabilized totality of the Four or the Earth, but verticalized and
pointing upwards because the Father, who has *breathed it out*, now
breathes it in. This means that to save mankind from damnation,
the lamb[116] (evoking the Vedic Agni, god of fire, symbolized by the

---

116 Fr.: *agneau*, "lamb." —Trans.

ram) is sacrificed on the altar, the shape of which is "square" because it symbolizes the city of man; stability and peace must reign there for life to develop harmoniously, sanctified by the martyrdom of the scapegoat. The inner flame, kindled by the gift of its life, accepted by Christ, is precisely the introjection of the fire of resentment, anger, and concupiscence that burns in the heart of the Fifth, the Prodigal Son, the lonely man without a home. Jalāl al-Dīn Rūmī tells us that one day, Jesus took shelter from the rain in a cave that was the den of a jackal and its young; a revelation came to him: "leave the jackal's den for its young cannot rest with you here." Jesus then exclaimed: "O Lord! there is a refuge for the jackal's young, but none for the son of Mary." And Rūmī comments: "If you have no home, what cause for concern is it? The grace and honor done specially to you by such a motivator to drive you on is a thousand thousand times more valuable than the sky, the earth, this world, the next world, and the Divine Throne all together."[117]

But the "fire of concupiscence," of envy and rebellion, is the very fire of desire and life, simultaneously capable of igniting the soul and also of becoming the energy of transmutation and *deificatio*. "Pure" and "fire" are the same word in Sanskrit. Saint Catherine understood this when she said that the fire of hell is only the light of God as felt by those who refuse it. The fire of the Holy Spirit warms the heart, transmutes the soul, exalts the intellect, divinizes life, but above all illuminates the spirit, Light being the supreme quintessence of Heavenly Fire. And Gilbert Durand adds: "It could be said that fire in the Prometheus myth is merely a symbolic sub-

---

117 Jalāl al-Dīn Rūmī, *Signs of the Unseen (Fihi ma Fihi)*, tr. W. M. Thackston, Jr. (Boulder: Shambhala, 1994).

stitute for the light-spirit."[118] And how is this "conversion" of fire expressed, as it descends from Heaven, is received by man according to his soul, and returns to Heaven as Resurrective Light?[119]

According to the hiero-geometric canon according to which the Egyptians carved and painted their myths, the descent and return of the triangular flame was symbolized in the "luminous delta," which expressed the descent of God's spirit among men, his death and resurrection. In fact, according to the myth transmitted by Plutarch, Osiris came into the world to civilize Egypt; having done so, he went south to civilize the rest of mankind, leaving governance to his sister Isis; on his return, his brother Set lured him into an ambush and he was killed by the 72 accomplices of the god of chaos. I have already shown elsewhere[120] that the mention of these 72 murderers of Osiris is not gratuitous—quite the contrary, for the god's "descent" to the horizon of man corresponds to the descent of the divine spirit from the upper summit of the luminous

---

118 Gilbert Durand, *The Anthropological Structures of the Imaginary*, tr. M. Sankey and J. Hatten (Brisbane: Boombana, 1999), p. 168. The author adds (p. 169): "Anthropologists confirm the role of fire as a symbol of the intellect; the use of fire marks 'the most important stage in the intellectualisation' of the cosmos and 'increasingly distances man from the animal condition.' For this spiritualist reason, fire is nearly always 'a present from God,' and is always endowed with an 'apotropaic' power. It is in its igneous aspect that the Uranian divinity appears to the apostles at Pentecost, to St. Bonaventure and to Dante. Fire is the 'living, thinking god' who, in the Aryan religions of Asia, has the names of Agni, Atar, and for the Christians, Christ. In Christian ritual, fire still plays an important part: the Paschal candle is kept for the whole year; and the letters on the cross stand for 'Igne Natura Renovatur Integra.'"

119 "...the element of fire, interpreted by a different Order of the image, is intimately linked to resurrection myths, either in its xylic origin for peoples who use friction tinder-boxes, or in the part that it plays in coction in numerous alchemies," writes Gilbert Durand (*op. cit*, p. 169).

120 Lima de Freitas, "Notes on Some Pentagonal 'Mysteries' in Egyptian and Christian Iconography," in *Fivefold Symmetry*, ed. István Hargittai (Singapore: World Scientific, 1992), pp. 307–332.

delta to the base of the triangle, polarized between two 36° angles. This base, correlating to the human world, is thus marked by the number 72, the sum of the two 36° angles. In fact, the dispersion of Osiris over the earth represents his sacrifice so that men may live; his "death" is simply the irradiation of his Word into the world, the disclosure and popularization of his message: for this to happen, he consents to "die" (to fall towards the horizontal) at the hands of the 72 accomplices of Set, who are the 72 nations of mankind, the 72 languages since the fall of the Tower of Babel (or the 70 — or 72?—languages used by the Creator to transmit the Torah),[121] as well as the 72 emissaries of Christ in the Gospel of Luke (10:1), the 72 translators of the Greek Bible (known as the Septuagint Bible, because the precise meaning of the geometric symbol has since been lost), and the 70 aspects (literally, "faces") of each word and even each letter of Sacred Scripture, according to Abraham ibn Ezra and the Kabbalist Joseph Gikatilla, and so on.

So, the god is dead. This means: the sense of his descent and his word has fallen prey to the general entropy that reigns in the manifested world; it has become scattered and degraded, and men have forgotten it, for most are deaf and blind and kill spirit and consciousness through ignorance and wickedness (through *avidya*, as the Hindus say, "absence of vision"). But divine consciousness, even buried in the petrified heart of man, cannot undergo absolute death, and the "remembrance" of celestial origin drives the soul towards the return to the "house of the Father." From the coffin springs a tree, according to the beautiful myth of Osiris. Isis, transformed into a swallow, discovers the tree and the god's body, which she takes back to Egypt. Osiris resuscitates from death. Springtime rites in Abydos celebrated his resurrection, which coincided with the beginning of the flooding of the Nile, a sign of the rebirth of life. They raised the Djed, a sort of "totemic" column embodying

---

121 Abécassis, *La lumière dans la pensée juive*.

Osirian energies, extinguished in the horizontal position and resurrected when the Djed stood upright. A large bas-relief in the Temple of Abydos shows the pharaoah Seti I in the process of symbolically raising the Djed, which is tilted to represent the passage from death to life. The tilted Djed makes an angle of 72° on the left side (measured from the ground), the "sinister" side of death, and an angle of 108° on the right side, the side where the pharaoh stands and where the verticalization of the symbolic column will soon take place. As we already know, 108 is the number of degrees from the upper summit of the luminous delta, and simultaneously the number of the divine spirit as it appears in the firmament of men and the celestial pole to which the god rises from death.

I have counted several examples in Egyptian iconography of a similar use of pentagonal angles in connection with resurrection myths.

V

Unus Mundus

The cooperation of conscious reasoning with the data of the unconscious is called the "transcendent function." This function progressively unites the opposites. Psychotherapy makes use of it to heal neurotic dissociations, but this function had already served as the basis of Hermetic philosophy for seventeen centuries. —C.G. Jung

Marie-Louise von Franz, as we've already mentioned, on the advice of her teacher Carl Gustav Jung, wrote a remarkable book in which numbers are studied as psychological entities; she came to a highly probable conclusion, which we have already mentioned, that numbers—especially the simplest whole numbers, which are in fact the most complex and difficult—have their roots in the deep unconscious and seem to respond to archetypal impulses.[122] But she goes further. She considers that, analogous to the constitution of matter, whose smallest grains—atoms, particles, sub-particles—seem to resolve themselves into *spins*, i.e., into *Numbers*, the psychic constitution of *Homo Sapiens* also seems to plunge its deepest roots into a kind of ocean of "psychoid" energies, from which occasionally emerge vibrations that I would call "primal," producing morphogenetic "orders" of the same nature as the *Numbers*. It is upon these primary—but unfathomable—structures that all conscious and unconscious psychic life seems to mold itself.

It would seem that there is here a kind of primordial communion between "matter" and "spirit," which would explain the incredible mystery of the accuracy, verified *a posteriori*, of certain totally abstract mathematical constructions, devoid of any experi-

---

122 von Franz, *Number and Time*.

mental or sensitive foundation, but which turn out to correspond to very fine and profound realities of the physics of the (let us say) "material" universe. It is as if certain structural and ordered speculations, elaborated by the human brain on the basis of logical and axiomatic premises devoid of contact with the world of experience and observation, came to correspond to facts of the physical world even before these were discovered, as fractal geometry has recently shown, by recovering certain mathematical "monsters" thought to be pure inventions, deemed futile by some as having no conceivable link with "reality." The *Urgrund*, or fundamental foundation of the universe as a whole—whether the "material" universe of astronomy and physics, or the "immaterial" universe of the psyche—would ultimately be one and the same *Urgrund*, whose most primordial common manifestation we discern in the form of *Numbers*. This idea, so dear to the Pythagoreans and alchemists, of an *Unus Mundus* in whose depths are at work *spins* or *Numbers* (a word which comes from the Latin *numen*, "head movement, assent, divine will, divine majesty, divinity"), an idea which the writings of Jung (who worked for a time with Wolfgang Pauli, Nobel Prize winner in physics) and the recent physics of David Bohm (whom I quoted above) seem to confirm, points towards the notion of a universal "psychoid" base from which emanate the archetypal dynamisms that go on to give rise to the fine "material" structure and form of worlds and things, or to shape and typify the "subjective" perceptions that man makes of the world—in other words, the religions, the conscious and unconscious networks of ideas and aspirations, the myths of civilizations and peoples.

This is perhaps to say that beneath the palpitation and diachrony of myth, or of certain myths, there is in all likelihood the radiant, "immobile" and achronic energy of a number, or of a numerical constellation; and that the very first conceptions of divinity and force, of causal chain and fatality, of origin and end, of repetition and mutation, of death and survival, etc., are probably made and remade in the secret crucible of numbers. This numeric core of myths, whose existence we suspect, would allow us to see in their genesis the manifestations of an abstract-concrete mold: "abstract," because the structuring, unchanging energy that manifests itself in the archetypal emergence of numbers most certainly operates outside space and time; and "concrete," because if number inhabits myth, it manifests itself paradoxically as "incarnate" number, engaged in the world in real actions which, while discharging the inviolable purity of number, are indissociable from it in its essence—its formal essence, certainly, but above all its formative or morphogenetic essence. Number, contemplated in this way, is not a truly "abstract" entity, but rather the blossoming of a psycho-physical energy that manifests itself at the same time, "synchronistically," in "both worlds," without there being any precedence of one manifestation over the other, for both, though separate, are but aspects of the same reality, the fruits of what might be described as acausal twinning.

This is probably the reason for the prestige of certain numbers that are repeated in the collective imagination, either in religion and ritual, or in their magical and superstitious degenerations, or in playful, poetic, literary, or artistic uses. But I believe that it is at the origins, *in illo tempore*, that we can best observe this *simultaneous blossoming* of myth and number, hence the exceptional interest of the "primitive" myths. This does not exclude the fact that we can sometimes find this archetypal phenomenon in a supremely elaborate form—and at the same time inextricably linked to the depths of a sacred emotion experienced at the roots of being in its conscious and unconscious totality—in certain myths that are simultaneously modern and immemorial: this is the case, of course, for the "synchronistic twinning" enacted by Dante, of the *Messo di Dio* and the number 515 that defines its hidden structure, the number of the invisible *spin*, beyond words, that nevertheless makes the image of the God-Man pronounceable and present in our world, elicits his Name, and resonates in his Word.

VI

The Triangle of Fire

…these technical models of circular rhythm, structured by the engram of the sexual gesture, will gradually free themselves from the pattern of eternal recommencement to reach a messianic meaning: that of the production of the Son, of which fire is a prototype. —Gilbert Durand[123]

When, after an interval of many years, I reread James Frazer's *Myths of the Origin of Fire*,[124] I was surprised to find a number of forgotten primitive myths that corroborated my hypotheses, sometimes in ways as striking as they were unexpected. I am referring here to the numbers 3, 4, and 5. Since fire has been "triangular" since time immemorial, it was only natural that three should play an important role in these myths. For the Ba-ila people of Zambia, fire was obtained from three birds, which they sought from God, and the quest lasted *thirty* years; according to a myth of the Zia Indians of New Mexico, *three* animals guarded the fire of the spider, creator of men and living beings; also in New Mexico, of the *three* animals, it was the *third*, the squirrel, that brought fire to the Navajo Indians, according to one of their myths, while for the Jicarilla Apaches, in northern New Mexico, the *third* was the brown crane; in a myth of the Uintah Utes, in Utah, it is a story of *three* birds going in search of fire. And let us not forget that, in the well-known Greek myth, Prometheus, who stole the celestial fire, suffered a sentence of *thirty* or *thirty thousand* years.

But when it comes to fire, we need to understand what we are talking about, because (as we already know) there are many dif-

---

123 Durand, *Anthropological Structures*, p. 390.
124 James G. Frazer, *Myths of the Origin of Fire* (London: Macmillan, 1930).

ferent kinds of fire. Myths often hint at this, and even declare it on occasion. The Trinitarian nature of fire is primarily concerned with celestial or divine fire. According to a myth of the Xipaya Indians, which I will examine in greater detail later, the hero Kumaphari, the abductor of fire, refuses to return the firebrand stolen from the "celestial" vulture in exchange for the "technical" fire obtained by rubbing sticks together; this proves that the object of his quest is the fire of heaven. Another myth, collected in Polynesia,[125] speaks of different types of fire, drawn from different parts of the body; the worst fire is that drawn from the feet or legs, while the sacred fire is drawn from the head. Several myths confirm that the "Spirit of Fire" comes from Heaven: from the sun, the moon, the stars (notably Castor and Pollux, the Pleiades, Canopus, and Mars), but also from the rainbow and divine lightning. The spirit Wun Lawa Makam, holder of fire in a Burmese Kachin myth, refused to give up the Spirit of Fire to the hero who had gone in search of it because, as he told him, the element would cause men too much harm; then, pressed by the hero, he conceded: "I cannot give you the Spirit of Fire, but I will tell you how to make fire."[126]

Gilbert Durand attaches decisive importance to the technical modalities of fire production in the symbolic modulation of the various imaginings. "There are," he writes, "two essential and obviously antithetical ways of producing fire: by percussion and by friction." The fire obtained by percussion "is psychologically related to the igneous arrow, the celestial and flamboyant stroke that constitutes lightning," linked to the Uranian and solar constellations of

---

125 Myth collected in the Marquesas Islands by E. Tregear, "Polynesian Folklore—Part II. The Origin of Fire," in *Transactions and Proceedings of the Royal Society of New Zealand*, vol. XX (Wellington: Lyon & Blair, 1887). See also Frazer, *Myths*.

126 Ch. Gilhodes, "Mythologie et religion des Katchins (Birmanie)," in *Anthropos*, vol. III (Fribourg: St. Paul, Anthropos-Institut, 1908). Quoted by Frazer, *Myths*.

the imaginal: an essentially purifying, "spiritual" fire, "isomorphic to the bird" in many myths of celestial fire, as we shall see later underlined in the myth of Kumaphari; this spiritual fire of sublimation and elevation which at the summit becomes light is also assimilated, as we have seen, to the word of God. In contrast, the more archaic, friction-based fire is (according to the same author) linked to the "quasi-semiological archetype of the union of opposites," and its roots lie in the rhythmic back-and-forth movement of the sexual gesture. Along with Eliade and Burnouf, Gilbert Durand links the wood of the tree, the cross, and the fire "in a context whose general pattern is rhythmic friction."[127] If Fire is a unifying element (as Xiuhtecuhtli, the Mexican god of fire, who sits at the "hearth" of the Universe, testifies), its modalities and "regimes" are nonetheless highly diversified, as is now becoming clear.

The Trinitarian essence of fire, and of celestial fire in particular, as found in many primitive myths that recount the quest for it, and which emphasize the number three in relation to the number of heroes and the time of the quest (for time, like an invisible flame, also *devours* beings and things), is a feature common to a wide variety of cultures, including Christianity. We all know that, according to the Joachimites, there will be a *third* and final age, that of the Holy Spirit, in other words, an age of Pentecostal *Fire*, whose symbolic vicar is a bird, the dove, once associated with the cult of Venus—note that for the aborigines of the Andaman Islands in Indonesia, it was the dove that brought fire to the ancestors.[128] In the Middle Ages, the hymn *Veni Sancte Spiritus* was accompanied by the sounding of trumpets, a shower of red petals and the flight of doves. Thus, the red flames of Pentecost descending from heaven, as well as the dove

---

127 Durand, *Anthropological Structures*, p. 381.

128 A. R. Brown, *The Andaman Islanders* (Cambridge: Cambridge University Press, 1922). Quoted by Frazer, *Myths*.

of the Annunciation (and of love) were associated with the cult of a time to come, comparable to a new—and final—golden age.[129]

As we have already noted, the link between fire and sex is also universal. In the myths of the origin of fire, as in many other mythical tales of the past or in folk traditions that still survive today—such as the feast of St. John at the summer solstice in many parts of Europe, during which jubilant couples leap over the flames and engage in propitiatory rites of marriage and fertility—fire is often seen to take on an overtly erotic hue. In a number of mythical accounts collected from "primitive" peoples, fire (seen above all in its operative aspect) is hidden in the genitalia, most often of women. For the natives of the Trobriand Islands, east of New Guinea, it was a woman, mother of the sun and moon, who gave birth to fire by taking it from between her legs; for the Tarumas of south-eastern French Guiana, fire emerged *in illo tempore* from the genital tract of the first woman, in the form of a fireball; also for the inhabitants of Dobu, an island off the coast of New Guinea, whose myth has it that an old woman made fire come out from between her legs, and that it was a snake that kept it there; etc. Fire can also be produced by a woman's skin, by the fingers of fire deities or by masturbation. This obviously evokes Pyramid Text 1248, which describes the primordial act of creation: Atum giving birth to himself by masturbating and bringing Shu and Tefnut into the world; or, according to another version, by spitting out (*ishish*) the first divine power, Shu—the Principle of air and space, symbolized by the feathers he wears on his head—and expectorating (*tfnt*) the second Principle,

---

129 Gilbert Durand, "Iconographie et symbolique du St-Esprit," in *Os Impérios do Espírito Santo e a Simbólica do Império, proceedings of the International Symposium on Symbology* (Angra do Heroismo, Pt.: Instituto Histórico da Ilha Terceira, 1985).

Tefnut with the lion's head, which most probably represents the element Fire.[130]

---

130 Lucie Lamy, *Egyptian Mysteries: New Light on Ancient Knowledge* (New York: Crossroad, 1981). According to yet another version, Atum created himself by projecting his heart and manifesting eight elemental principles which, added to himself, gave rise to the Nine, the Great Ennead of Heliopolis: Shu and Tefnut, then Geb (Earth), Nut (Heaven), finally Osiris and Isis, Set and Nephthys, principles of cyclical life and renewal, death and rebirth. "None of these entities is separate from him, Atum," declares one of the Pyramid Texts (1655). A "Coffin Text" from the Middle Kingdom (after 2040 BCE) adds further details: a deceased person identifying himself successively with each of the deities says: "I was the soul of Shu who is *in the flame*, the fire that Atum produced *with his hand when he masturbated.*" Lucie Lamy adds this comment (p. 9): "The male seed is here considered a catalyst, or in alchemical terms, a 'styptic fire': a coagulating agent which causes the 'first earth' or 'primordial hill' to emerge from the undefined cosmic substance of the Nun [the cosmic ocean, the incomprehensible Power of the infinite source of the Universe, outside space-time]. This initial condensing agent is symbolized by the spermatozoon which coagulates the female albuminous liquid exactly as the heat of a flame does the white of an egg."

Note that the offspring of this essentially igneous creative act already conceals all the complexity and richness of the world-creating numbers: From the One (Atum) comes the Two (Shu and Tefnut), making the first Divine Triad (Three), which begets first Earth and Heaven and then Osiris-Isis and Seth-Nephtys, i.e. successively the square (4) formed by Space and Fire with Earth and Heaven, closing the "metaphysical" series of Formitive Principles, and the two "hominized" pairs Osiris-Isis and Seth-Nephtys. The two pairs Space-Fire and Earth-Heaven (Heaven probably corresponding to Celestial Water, the archetype of the lower waters) added to the First Principle, Atum, form the Pentad: the 5, which immediately takes on human form and polarizes. The whole constitutes the 9, the "number of generation," which appears doubled in the Pyramid Texts ("*The king comes out from between the thighs of the divine Nine*" or "*from between the thighs of the two divine Nines*"). But this duplication leaves the Principles intact in their order and essence: $2 \times 9 = 18$, this number still being the Great Ennead ($18 = 1 + 8 = 9$). Another observation to be made concerns the "trinity" of the creative act, homologated to the power of "fire," which is initially sexual. Indeed, versions of the Heliopolitan myth speak of three forms of creation: ejaculation, spitting, and "heart projection." We have here a striking analogy with the primitive myths mentioned by Frazer, where they refer to the existence of several fires,

The fire-drill concentrates within itself many of the mythical forms of flame production, as its operation evokes sexual intercourse. It is true that this primitive instrument produces the banal, utilitarian fire whose "technology" the god of Burma's Kachins agreed to reveal; but we must not forget that even in banal fire there shines something of the divine fire from which it originates. This explains the ceremonies of "rejuvenation" and the sacralization of fire in more elaborate traditional cultures. Frazer's book describes the rites "by which to this day the Brahman fire-priest (*Agnihotra*) and his wife between them kindle the sacred fire by means of the fire-drill. On the night before fire is made, the priest is given charge of the plunger or upper part of the fire-drill (*arani*) and his wife is given charge of the lower part, and husband and wife sleep with these parts at night, 'the process of fire-making symbolizing coition.' Next morning they together kindle the sacred fire; the man holds the plunger firmly so that the point cannot leave the hole in the base-board, while his wife causes it to revolve by pulling the cord wound about it until fire is produced and communicated to the tinder. Both husband and wife are subject to special taboos while they are engaged in the performance of this sacred duty."[131]

---

originating from various parts of the human body. And we also have three essential levels of the creative act, relating to what we call body, soul, and spirit. Three divine "emissions" (semen, the "styptic" or coagulating fire of desire and conception; saliva, the Word of wisdom that fills space and the heart; and the "projection of the heart," the heat and light of divine love that warms and illuminates) through which the god, the "hidden treasure," reveals himself to himself in creating worlds and creatures. Note that the word Three (*Khemt*) is written hieroglyphically with the phallus, seminal power, in the sense of "to think," or "to conceive" (Ger. *bedenken*). There is a curious allusion to the Ennead in the Siberian myth of the Pamir, cited by Mircea Eliade, *Forgerons et alchimistes* (Paris: Flammarion, 1977), which features a celestial Ironworker, a civilizing hero sent to earth to teach men metallurgy, with his daughter and *nine* sons.

131　Frazer's indications are taken from W. Crooke, *Religion and Folklore of Northern India* (Oxford: Oxford University Press, 1926).

Moreover, the theft of celestial fire is sometimes compensated for, in certain myths,[132] by the suspension of certain sexual taboos and the consent given to erotic excesses. A fine example of the sexualization of fire is the myth of the Marind-Anim, from the southern coast of New Guinea, in which fire is born of the loving embrace between a man called Uaba and his wife Ualiuamb; the fire bursts forth when a spirit tries to separate them. According to P. Wirtz, who studied the same people of New Guinea, until recently the solemn lighting of the fire was accompanied by sexual orgies, which were supposed to be essential for the conservation of this element.

But to my mind, the most extraordinary myth that I discovered in the book *Myths of the Origin of Fire* is that of the Xipaya Indians, inhabitants of the Xingu Basin in central Brazil.[133] Here is the story in a nutshell:

---

132 For example, in a myth of the Coushatta Indians of North America, collected by John R. Swanton, *Myths and Tales of the Southeastern Indians*, Bureau of American Ethnology, Bulletin 88 (1929). Quoted by Frazer, *Myths*.

133 This myth was collected by Curt Nimuendaju, "Bruchstücke aus Religion und Überlieferung der Šipáia-Indianer," *Anthropos*, vol. XIV–XV (Fribourg: St. Paul, Anthropos-Institut, 1919–1920), p. 1015. Quoted by Frazer, *Myths*, pp. 128–129.

According to a recent study by Anna Curtenius Roosevelt, anthropologist at the American Museum of Natural History in New York, published in the excellent catalog of the exhibition *Brasil, Nas Vésperas do Mundo Moderno*, organized by the National Commission for the Commemoration of Portuguese Discoveries (Lisbon, 1992), "the archaeological record of the Amazon bears witness in recent prehistory to the existence of complex societies along the river's alluvial plains. The millennium preceding the conquest is characterized by the generalization of true stylistic horizons" in the production of ceramics. The same author goes on to say that "the archaeological phases of low-resource interfluvial areas seem to lack the complexity and cultic grandeur of the phases identified in the alluvial plains, with a few important exceptions: interfluvial regions characterized by sedimentary deposits that enriched the soils with nutrients, such as the Caribbean coast in Venezuela; *the upper and middle Xingu, in Brazil*; and the foot of the Andes in the upper Amazon and western Orinoco." According to the most recent research, the

Once a vulture (*Gavião de Anta*) came flying with a firebrand in his talons and mocked Kumaphari [the Younger, a great tribal hero,] because he had no fire. Then the hero pondered how he could get possession of the fire. He observed that the vulture, after perching on a tree, flew down and gorged on carrion. The sight suggested a plan to Kumaphari. He laid himself down on the ground, died and rotted. The vulture came with other birds of prey to devour the putrid flesh, but he left his fire on a tree-stump so far away that Kumaphari could not reach it. The birds ate up the flesh and left nothing over but the bones. Then Kumaphari turned himself into a stag and died again. The other birds of prey came to devour the dead stag, but the vulture was suspicious. [...] At last, Kumaphari opened his eyes a little. The vulture perceived it and cried, "See! Didn't I tell you that he was still alive?' So saying he took his firebrand and flew away with it. At last Kumaphari lay down on a great slab of stone and died yet again. He spread out his arms, and they penetrated like roots into the ground and then came forth again in the shape of two bushes, each of them with five branches springing from a single point of the stem. When the vulture came to devour the carrion, says he to himself, "In these forked branches is a nice place for my fire." So saying he put the firebrand in Kumaphari's hand. The hero clutched

---

iconography of these Amazon basin cultures reveals the great importance accorded to the human figure, which supplants that of zoomorphic images. Male images are rarer than female ones, and mostly depict shamans/chiefs. "We find them," writes Anna C. Roosevelt, "seated on stools, wearing rattles like those of the rattlesnake, characteristic hats, bags on their backs; they present themselves as figures with an *alter-ego*, carrying another person or animal on their shoulders. It is assumed that the *alter-ego* image represents the transformation of a shaman into a spirit helper, through drug-induced trances."

it and jumped up: the fire was in his possession. But the vulture shrieked out: "You claim to be the son of your father, Kumaphari the Elder, and yet you do not know how to make fire! The way is to lay sticks of *urukus* in the sun and then to twirl them one in the other." "Very good," quoth Kumaphari, "now I know that also; but I prefer to keep the firebrand, you shall not have it again."

First of all, in this extraordinary myth, we note the presence of the number three, namely in the hero's three attempts to steal fire from the vulture;[134] these three attempts are as many "deaths" of Kuma-

---

134 Frazer's mention of the Portuguese-language designation *gavião de anta* ("tapir-hawk" or black caracara) raises some doubts, since in the myth we are examining, it certainly refers to a vulture (the *urubu*, a very common species of vulture in tropical America). This is probably a local idiomatic expression. But it is no less interesting when you consider the symbolic importance of the hawk (*falco nisus*), especially in Egyptian mythology, where this bird of prey represented the orbit of the sun in the sky; Ra, the sun, was represented by a hawk-headed man surmounted by a disc rimmed by the uræus; moreover, a hawk with a man's head was the hieroglyph for the soul. The vulture, for its part, has a very rich imaginary world, of which we will only highlight its association, in the Mayan calendar, with the storms of the dry season, which ensure the renewal of vegetation. By feeding on rotting corpses, it purifies the air and the earth. In many South American Indian myths, the vulture is the first possessor of fire and (as with the Bambara of Sub-Saharan Africa) a symbol of fertility and abundance, in all aspects of wealth: vital, material and spiritual. See *Dictionnaire des symboles*, ed. Jean Chevalier (Paris: Robert Laffont, 1969). This clearly prefigures the gifts of the Holy Spirit, the essence of which is unknown.

Furthermore, the word *uruku* or *urucu* pronounced by the vulture ("*to lay sticks of* urukus *in the sun and then to twirl them one in the other*" to produce the common fire) refers to a bush of the Amazonian flora, whose *red* flowers with abundant pollen are used as a basic blush. Gilbert Durand, who visited the Amazon and kindly passed on this very interesting piece of information to me, adds that he "tried the shimmering powder of this pollen, which is very tenacious, very flamboyant, and which the Amazonians use to adorn their bodies with skilful ornaments." Could there be a phonetic link between *urucu* (the "burning" bush) and *urubu* the vulture? As far as affinities of meaning are concerned, there's no denying it!

phari, eaten by birds of prey successively as a man, as a deer, and partially transformed into a bush. Throughout the world, the initiation of shamans almost invariably involves the horrific suffering they undergo when an animal (beast, bird, reptile, etc.) or a demonic being deprives them of their powers — or when a demonic being skins and devours them. Eliade mentions several stories in which the shaman, in a dream or hallucination related to his initiation, witnesses the destruction of his own body, butchered by demons. One of these tales, collected among the Yakuts, describes how the "Mother Bird of Prey" cut the shaman into small pieces; another Siberian myth recounts the cutting of the shaman (an *Avam-Samoyed*) into pieces, which are then thrown into a cauldron, where they are cooked for *three* years.[135]

Kumaphari does not escape the ordeal: he is truly a shaman. His succession of "deaths" also represents a regression, a gradual renunciation of the characteristics and mental forms of acculturated man. Only by descending to the least hominized levels of consciousness (the vegetal or vegetative level), when the shaman has ceased thought, inner monologue, and even the "voice" of instinct, can he steal fire from the vulture. In many myths, from those of recent prehistory to the most elaborate, there is an important link between the sacrifice of the hero, the god (or virgin, buried as the seed is buried), and the fertility of fields and crops. Osiris is doubly "vegetalized," firstly in the immense tree that grows from his tomb, according to the myth transmitted by Plutarch, and secondly during the ceremonies celebrated in the temples that guarded his relics: a bed filled with humus and sown with grains of wheat was ritually watered, and a golden image of the god was placed on it. Purification by fire also corresponded to the renewal of vegetation and the resurrection of life. The mythical figure of the Phoenix,

---

135 Eliade, *Forgerons et alchimistes*; see also by the same author *Le Chamanisme et les techniques archaïques de l'extase* (Paris: Payot, 1974), p. 50.

so dear to alchemists, expresses the flight of a life regenerated and sublimated by the ordeal of fire.

As for Kumaphari's death as a stag, it is interesting to note the close symbolic contiguity between the myth of the Brazilian Xipaya and other myths far removed from the Xingu basin, including the Christian legend of St. Hubert. According to this legend, the crucified Christ appeared to Hubert between the antlers of the stag he was hunting, a vision that struck him, converted him, and made him a saint. Iconographic representations of the miracle—of which Dürer's famous engraving is a prestigious example—traditionally show five branches or "horns" on either side of the stag's head. This is precisely the number indicated by the Xipaya myth. The same Brazilian myth also sheds light on the symbolic basis of the number, as it actually refers to the fingers of the hands. The stag's antlers certainly mark the "vegetation" of the shaman, a token of the periodic and resurrectionary renewal to which I alluded, but they also herald the numbers 5 and 5, which appear in the third moment of the myth and already herald the famous 515 of Dante's *Purgatorio!*

Kumaphari's hands are thus transformed into bushes, each with five branches. The vulture misunderstands and places the magic firebrand in the hero's hand. This makes the number 5 the bearer of celestial fire. Is this in line with traditional symbolism? We already know that the 3, as an equilateral triangle, reflects the divine tri-unity in its principial purity; but, as soon as it manifests itself to man, as Ezekiel's first vision testifies, the geometric symbol of this theophany becomes a less "perfect" triangle, for the divine essence of the Three has descended into the gross manifestation of our world of space, time, and aging. This "less perfect" triangle was the sacred triangle of the Egyptians, known to us (albeit in a desacralized form) as the Pythagorean triangle. We are thus confronted with the 3—4—5 inequality, whose ligaments hide the divine unity beneath the medial equality of the two polarizations $3+4=5$, only perceptible in the magnifying mirror of its square powers: $9+16=25$ or $25=25$. Here we are, then, confronted with the roots of 25, the most direct illustration of which (essentially anthropomorphic) is given by man's two symmetrical hands.

Two hands, therefore duality. And this duality manifests itself not only anatomically, but also in the separation of the "waters" by the middle horizon (as we saw above) making man a *"compost"* of "Earth" and the "celestial Fire" that gives him life. The oldest known religious text is inscribed in the Unas Pyramid at Saqqara (5th dynasty, c. 2,400 BCE), and reads something like this: "The body belongs to the earth, the spirit belongs to heaven." And indeed, man (the 5) is made up of a "spirit" (the 3) and a "body" (the 2), in other words, he is masculine and feminine, solar and lunar, composed of "good" and "evil," and so on. From the outset, five has been a duality, an addition, a marriage, a compromise, a conflict, a tension, made up of love and evil, light and darkness. This is why the symbolic geometry of the pentagon detaches the "head triangle" (or the "luminous delta" of the ancient builders), leaving the two remaining vertices "below."

This figure symbolizes the human being, made up of a "triangular" spirit and a "binary" body; the latter is merely the "vessel" of the higher "fire" (the invisible fire, the breath of God) from which it receives its life force. A very interesting myth from the Cora Indians of Mexico, collected in the first decade of the 20th century by an expedition to Nayarit, relates that in primordial times the iguana possessed fire, but having quarreled with his wife and mother-in-law, he withdrew to heaven, taking the fire with him. "Thus there was no more fire on earth, because the iguana had carried it all away and kept it hidden up aloft."[136] Here we have the triangle

---

136 Frazer, *Myths*, pp. 136-138. Myth collected by Konrad Theodor Preuss, *Die Nayarit Expedition* (Leipzig: B. G. Teubner, 1912).

of fire, made up of the iguana, his wife and his mother-in-law, of which the iguana is the upper "vertex"; what remains of the anthropomorphic "pentagon," deserted by celestial fire, is in fact only the lower duality, corporeal and earthly, devoid of the flame of life. The myth goes on to tell how creatures painfully felt the lack of fire, so the old and the young gathered and deliberated for three days without eating, drinking or sleeping. Finally, after five days, they knew that fire was in heaven. This progression of numbers, which starts in 2 (two groups of people: the old and the young), continues in 3 (three days of fasting and watchfulness), and ends in 5 (five days of reflection until the realization of the place—"heaven"—where the fire is hidden), is extremely eloquent. We can see that the base of the triangle, in other words, the duo composed of the iguana's wife and mother-in-law, embodies the presence of the social community within consciousness and is transformed into two groups of people, the "young" (the "wife") and the "old" (the "mother-in-law"), i.e., the active physical body, in the present, and the mnemonic "body" rich in the teachings of the past. The 3 days of fasting (and no *sleep*) mark the price of awakening consciousness and the sacrificial deadline, while at the same time defining the triadic essence of fire; the acquisition of this consciousness is complete at the end of five days, i.e. 3 + 2. Five thus represents the "center of the four," 4 being the figure of the more or less arrested agreement obtained through reflection (consciousness perceiving the celestial nature of fire), an agreement which must nevertheless somehow go beyond the stage of a simple "addition" or collage of the elements of the problem and "center" itself in a single, self-conscious act of understanding; this centralizing unification is given by pentagonal crystallization. In other words, the strenuous efforts of the two age groups—symbolizing the "young," "somatic" vitality that springs from instinctive and intuitive synapses, combined with the mnemonic heritage accumulated over time (the "old men")—succeed in releasing from the collective unconscious the archetypal figure of totality: the harmonious, organic whole composed of the "earthly" body and the "celestial fire," crystallized in the pentagram.

The rest of the Cora myth recounts the efforts of several seekers to climb up to the fire in heaven and bring it back down to earth. There are five of these efforts, with only the fifth (accomplished by the opossum)[137] being successful. The *fifth*, as we know, is the "son," a cunning, daring, transgressive young man. He grabs a brand of celestial fire with his tail and flees, persecuted by the old celestial guardian; the latter catches him and beats him up; too late, the opossum had already thrown the firebrand down to earth. He too falls into the abyss and dies, but the inhabitants of the earth give him back his life by wrapping him in their blankets, prepared to collect the fire from heaven. Yet the fire spreads disastrously everywhere; it is finally the Earth goddess, begged by the men, who extinguishes it by sprinkling it with her milk. The final part of the myth is very interesting, but its analysis would take us far afield. In any case, let us remember in this beautiful Mexican myth the double five: the first, "passive" (5 days of reflection), the second, "active" (5 attempts to reach heaven); and also the hero's death and resurrection, under the sign of the shroud that keeps the warmth and hatches the egg of new life.

The legendary hero of the Xipaya Indians of Brazil, mentioned above, also dies before finding the "geometry" of the Fire-Man, i.e. the pentagonal figure of the double Five (the two hands, twice five fingers or five branches): an anthropomorphic figure in which the upper triangle of the Spirit "marries" the lower "binary" body. After his efforts to steal the vulture's fire, undertaken either in his human body or in the form of a deer—where already, in the animal's

---

137 A name borrowed from Algonquin, common to various American marsupials, which provide a highly prized fur. Of course, the stains on its fur are the remnants of the blows received during the flight of the celestial fire…

antlers, albeit unexplained, there is the outline of the "supernatural" structure of the "two times five"— Kumaphari invests all his power in his hands, transformed into bushes, and finally snatches the celestial fire: henceforth, he is simultaneously Earthly Man and Heavenly Man, as was Osiris, the son of Geb, Earth, and Nut, Heaven, as was Jesus Christ, Son of God and Mary. His "hieroglyph" thus arises of its own accord, as a sign of "igneous unity" (the One) remade within earthly or human duality (the double five), i.e.: 5 1 5.

VII

The Lost Letter

O living flame of love
That tenderly wounds my soul
In its deepest center! Since
Now you are not oppressive,
Now consummate! if it be your will:
Tear through the veil of this sweet encounter!
O sweet cautery,
O delightful wound!
O gentle hand…
—St. John of the Cross

The "fingerlike" nature of the five brings up other important points. They concern certain myths from recent or ancient prehistory, equivalents of which can be found in our own traditions, thus attesting to the universality of archetypal impulses, which are indifferent to the cultural milieu and the abysses of time and space. I will briefly mention a few stories from recent prehistory in which fire is born from the fingers of the hand, and in which there is particular mention of a sixth finger with specifically igneous properties. In the western islands of the Torres Strait, between Australia and New Guinea, a myth has been collected (paradigmatic of a whole group of similar myths) according to which humans once possessed six fingers instead of five; in particular, there was an old woman named Serkar who used the sixth finger she had in her right hand as a coal to light fire whenever she needed it. The hero of this myth, incarnate in the "long-necked lizard," cut off her prodigious finger with his tooth and returned to the world of men. Since that day, there has been a gap in man's hand, between his thumb and index finger.[138]

This missing fire-bearing finger once again raises the question of the "geometry" of "magical" (or celestial) fire. It corresponds to the firebrand placed in Kumaphari's bush hand by the vulture in the Xipaya myth, as a sixth finger with marvellous and fearsome powers. *This transforms the 1 in the symbolic equation 515 into the sixth finger,* which can therefore be read as 51.5 or 5.15, depending on whether the right hand is "read" to the right or left in the number. Remember that 515 can be obtained by dividing the number 927 (total of the internal angles of the "reflected" luminous delta) by 180, the value of the internal angles of any non-"inverted" triangle; in reality, the precise result of this division is 5.15. Of course, the decimal point is of no importance in "kabbalistic" calculations, where only symbolic valence is of interest. Yet we discover, thanks to myths from Brazil and New Guinea, that even the "dot" can be charged with symbolic valence! Finally, the loss of the "sixth" finger would correspond to the disappearance of the 1 in the 515, i.e., to the contraction of the androgynous and unfathomable number of the God-Man, reduced to the number 55 of banal man, in his inescapable sexual polarity, in his irremissible duality: in short, the totally mortal man deserted by celestial fire. The Savior, the Paraclete, the 515, is the Envoy from Heaven who brings to earth this "finger

---

138 See Frazer, *Myths*, pp. 25–27. This myth is mentioned in *Reports of the Cambridge Anthropological Expedition to Torres Straits*, vol. VI (Cambridge, 1908). In another version of this myth, quoted in the same work, collected on one of the islands close to New Guinea (Daudai), the hero cuts off Serkar's entire right hand, where she had a sixth finger between the index finger and thumb. According to a myth of the Maori of New Zealand, the hero's old grandmother—a true rule-breaking trickster "who loves to deceive and wrong others"—produces fire by pulling on her fingernails (Frazer, *ibid.*, p. 71). Frazer mentions eight myths in which fire springs from the fingers (1), or from a sixth finger or the index finger of the right hand (5) or the left hand (1), or from the fingernails and toenails (1).

of fire" that men have lost, igniting in those capable of receiving it the forgotten flame.[139]

It is also worth noting that in Kabbalistic tradition — particularly that inspired by the *Sefer HaTemunah*, the "Book of the Form" (referring to the shape of the characters) or the "Book of the Image" (of God) — we find a reference to a truncated letter or (in another version) the loss of a letter of the Hebrew alphabet. In our period of the universe, it says, "a letter of the Torah is missing." Gershom Scholem points out in one of his works that "this statement was interpreted in two ways. In one view, which seems to have been shared by the author of the [*Sefer HaTemunah*], a certain letter of the alphabet is in its present form incomplete and faulty, whereas it was perfect in the preceding *shemitah* and will again be so in the next."[140] (Let us explain that for the unknown author of the *Temunah*, the *shemitoth* are 7,000-year cycles which regulate the history of the universe according to the *sefiroth*, our "creation" being situated in the second of these cycles.) "Since every letter represents a concentration of divine energy, it may be inferred from the deficiency of its present visible form that the power of severe judgment, which sets its stamp on our world, impedes the activity of the hidden lights and forces and prevents them from being fully manifested. The limitations of our life under the rule of the visible Torah show that something is missing in it which will be made good only in another state of being. In the view of these Kab-

---

139 Siberian Yurak-Samoyed shamans have a seven-fingered glove. Mircea Eliade classifies this glove among the manifestations of the mystical number 7, which, attributed to the branches of the Cosmic Tree with 7 planetary heavens, "is certainly due to influences of Mesopotamian origin." Compare Eliade, *Chamanisme*, pp. 224–225. It is curious, to say the least, that the Russian-Jewish painter Marc Chagall painted a "Self-Portrait with Seven Fingers," dated 1913 (in the Stedelijk Museum, Amsterdam).

140 Gershom Scholem, *On the Kabbalah and Its Symbolism*, tr. Ralph Manheim (New York: Schocken, 1965), p. 80.

balists," Scholem adds, "the faulty letter of the Torah is the consonant *shin*, which we write with three prongs, ❡, but which in its complete form should have four [...] In the other view, which is far more radical, a letter is actually lacking in our alphabet; in our aeon this letter is not manifested and hence does not occur in our Torah. The implications of this view are obvious. The original divine alphabet and hence the complete Torah contained 23 letters, one of which has become invisible to us and will again be made manifest only in the next *shemitah*. It is only because this letter is missing that we read positive and negative ordinances in the Torah. Every negative aspect is connected with this missing letter of the original alphabet."[141] The same author reports, in a note, "an interesting parallel to these inferences" in a Christian tradition, according to which "three chapters in the Bible are missing and exist only in the hands of the magicians." Possession of these chapters would grant supernatural powers.[142]

Remarkably, the "secret value" of the letter *shin* according to Abellio's key[143] is 180, i.e., the number of degrees of the internal angles of the triangle. *Shin* is thus linked to the symbolism of fire.[144] This irresistibly evokes the "missing finger" of archaic New Guinea

---

141 Scholem, *On the Kabbalah*, pp. 80 – 81.

142 Scholem, *On the Kabbalah*, p. 82 n. 2. Scholem indicates that he found this tradition mentioned in Friedrich von Oppeln-Bronikowski, *Der Schwarzkünstler Cagliostro nach zeitgenössischen Berichten* (Dresden: C. Reissner, 1922), p. 98. The reference to the lost chapters of the Bible is found in a passage on Cagliostro by Elisa von der Recke, which must have been written in 1779 in Mitau. The number *three* (the three missing chapters) can be seen as a "triangular" reading of the "fingerlike" One, since the missing "finger" is "fire," and fire is triangular.

143 This key links each letter to one of the 22 regular polygons that can be written in the 360 degrees of a circle, whose central angle is a whole number of degrees.

144 This link is confirmed by the fact that *Shin* is the first letter of the root SA, "fire."

myths, all the more so as the letter *shin* looks rather like a hand—
and we know the high significance accorded by Jewish tradition
to the fingers of the hand. Scripture says: "You shall make bars of
shittim wood, five on one side of the tabernacle and five on the
other, and a bar in the middle."[145] The middle finger has two fingers
on either side. According to the *Zohar*, the two fingers immediately
touching the middle finger, the index and ring fingers, are an integral part of the middle bar. This is why the priest raises these three
fingers when he blesses the people.[146] Perhaps we should conclude

---

145 Paraphrase of Exodus 26:26–28.—Trans.

146 See Abellio, *La Bible, document chiffré*, vol. 1, p. 105. Abellio refers to the *Zohar*.
In a note, the same author adds, with regard to the quoted text of Scripture,
an essential remark for our investigation, which "also highlights the importance of the number 55 = secret value of 10, symbolized by man's two hands.
If, as the text indicates, we break down 5–5 according to 131 (right hand)
and 131 (left hand), we obtain two key numbers in the sephirotic construction: 131 firstly, the synthesis of the fourth and fifth sephiroth, and above all
131 × 2 = 262, the value of the *Shekinah*, one of the most important entities of
the *Zohar*."

For our part, we will point out firstly that 131 and 262 are symmetrical numbers, like 515; secondly, that the value of the two hands during
the first *shemitah* (and the one to come) would be, according to the same
calculation, 131 (left hand) + 141 (right hand) = 272 (again a symmetrical
number), which can be read as 2 × 72, implying an inversion of the reflected angles of the base of the luminous delta, restoring to the "reflection"
of the "Divine Head" its intact value, undistorted by the "Fall." Note that
2 × 72 = 144 = 4 × 36, and that the next "step" in the progression of 36 is
5 × 36 = 180, the value of the triangle. Note also that duplication of the value
of the base angles of the luminous delta results in duplication of the vertex
angle, enabling the following operation: (2 × 72) + (2 × 108) = 144 + 216 =
360, the value that reconstitutes the entire circle. This same value of 360°
can be obtained from the sum 272 by considering the cleavages 2 and 72;
multiplied, as we have just seen, these two figures produce the result 144
and lead, therefore, to the reconstitution of the circle in its completeness. In
other words, when man still had a "sixth finger," he maintained direct, "operative" contact with the fire of God, i.e., with the "non-inverted" luminous
delta and the circle of the Whole. If we repeat the same operations with the

that during the first *shemita*, or creation cycle, he did so with *four* fingers raised.

In the myth of the Xipaya, we thus detect a forerunner of the symbolic content of the symmetries of the 5. It is thanks to the bushes into which the shaman Kumaphari's hands are transformed that he acquires the fire of the vulture. From then on, the five and fire are intimately associated in myth and symbology, the human-five and the divine-fire. It is also worth noting that pentagonal symmetries, thanks to the extraordinary properties of both the number *phi* and the logarithmic spiral, and the proliferation of golden numbers triggered by the pentagon and pentagram, are linked not only to mythology—as in the case of the myth of Osiris transmitted by Plutarch, from which an unexpected pentagonal reading can be made that closely adheres to the text[147]—but also to the recent discoveries of quasicrystals, hitherto considered impossible, which have recently overturned the physics of solids and rehabilitated the geometry of the Five, so dear to the Egyptians and Pythagoreans of the distant past; they have also recently been linked to the biological roots of life, according to the work and insights of researchers such as neuro-cybernetician Jean-Claude Perez, according to whom the relative proportions of bases in genes are controlled by the Fibonacci and Lucas numbers—in other words, by the golden ratio.[148]

Finally, we have seen how the transformation of Kumaphari

"actual" number of fingers on both hands, i.e., with the double value 131, or 262, we obtain $2 \times 62 = 124$, a number which, added to 216 (double the 108° angle of the vertex of the "luminous" triangle) produces the result 340, i.e. a number far from the totality of the circle. This distance is 20°, a figure that "amplifies" the duality inherent in the condition of man separated from "fire."

147 See page 97, note 120.

148 J. C. Perez, "Integers neural network systems (INNS) using resonance properties of a Fibonacci's chaotic 'golden neuron,'" International Joint Conference on Neural Networks, 1990. San Diego, USA.

into a deer evokes, in the depths of the Brazilian forest, the Christic sacrifice that converted St. Hubert and how, by transforming his hand into a bush that *seizes* the fire of heaven, the shaman of the Xipaya tribe not only announces the vision of Moses on Mount Horeb, but also posits the "hiero-geometry" of 515, *Messo di Dio.* Man's vocation is to become a "star," as the ancient inscription on the Pyramid of Unas says; and this star emits five rays of light, like the fingers of his hand.

VIII

Fire in the Bush

He enters all beings
The migratory bird
And makes himself present in them
Like fire in rubbed sticks…
He is the Supreme Bird
Resplendent with the light
Of ten million suns
By whom all things have been penetrated…
To know this is to conquer death.
> —Hamsa Upanishad

I would now like to place side-by-side the visions of Moses on Mount Horeb and the myth of the origin of fire of the Xipaya Indians, which we have just examined. Let us open the Old Testament to chapter 3 of Exodus. There we read:

1   Now Moses kept the flock of Jethro his father in law, the priest of Midian: and he led the flock to the backside of the desert, and came to the mountain of God, even to Horeb.

2   And the angel of IHVH appeared unto him in a flame of fire out of the midst of a bush: and he looked, and, behold, the bush burned with fire, and the bush was not consumed.

3   And Moses said, I will now turn aside, and see this great sight, why the bush is not burnt.

4   And when IHVH saw that he turned aside to see, God called unto him out of the midst of the bush, and said, Moses, Moses. And he said, Here am I.

> 5 And he said, Draw not nigh hither: put off thy shoes from off thy feet, for the place whereon thou standest is holy ground.
>
> 6 Moreover he said, I am the God of thy father, the God of Abraham, the God of Isaac, and the God of Jacob. And Moses hid his face; for he was afraid to look upon God.

He will go up to Mount Sinai after leading his people out of Egypt. "In the third month, when the children of Israel were gone forth out of the land of Egypt, the same day came they into the wilderness of Sinai," we read in chapter 19 of Exodus; and there the people of Israel camped before the mountain. Note the presence of the number three in the date, marking the day of the theophany.[149] Indeed, the number three often appears in connection with the passage of time necessary for the completion of a temporal cycle, only after which the extraordinary event can take place. This stems from the fact that any manifestation is only possible with the cooperation of three forces; geometrically, the triangle is the first "possible" polygon in our world (for a two-sided polygon, let alone a one-sided one, is unthinkable).

As soon as Moses reaches the foot of the mountain, he ascends "unto Elohim." The number three recurs again, with the same character of necessity, postulating the preliminary delay or the three indispensable conditions for any departure, when IHVH says to Moses: "Go unto the people, and sanctify them to day and to morrow, and let them wash their clothes, and be ready against the third day" (Ex. 19:10–11). On the third day, it came to pass "in the morning, that there were thunders and lightnings, and a thick cloud upon the mount, and the voice of the trumpet exceeding loud; so that

---

149 One interpretation of Exodus 19:1, "In the third month, [...] the same day," is the third day of the third month. St. Jerome, *Sancti Eusebii Hieronymi Epistulæ* (Vindobonae: F. Tempsky; Lipsiae: G. Freytag, 1912) vol. 2, ep. 78:14, p. 62. —Trans.

all the people that was in the camp trembled. And Moses brought forth the people out of the camp to meet with God; and they stood at the nether part of the mount. And mount Sinai was altogether on a smoke, because IHVH descended upon it in fire: and the smoke thereof ascended as the smoke of a furnace, and the whole mount quaked greatly. And when the voice of the trumpet sounded long, and waxed louder and louder, Moses spake, and God answered him by a voice" (Ex. 19:16–19).

It was on the mountain that Moses received the tablets of the law, "the Law and the Rule, written by God": "And Moses went up into the mount, and a cloud covered the mount. And the glory of the Lord abode upon mount Sinai, and the cloud covered it six days: and the seventh day he called unto Moses out of the midst of the cloud. And the sight of the glory of IHVH was like devouring fire on the top of the mount in the eyes of the children of Israel. And Moses went into the midst of the cloud, and gat him up into the mount: and Moses was in the mount forty days and forty nights" (Ex. 24:15–18). He received the two tablets of the testimony, "tables of stone, written with the finger of God" (Ex. 31:18), tablets which "were the work of God, and the writing was the writing of God, graven upon the tables" (Ex. 32:16).

But during Moses' forty-day absence, the people had returned to idolatry and made a golden calf, before which they celebrated and danced. Moses, seized with anger, broke the tablets. In chapter 34, IHVH told Moses to carve two tablets of stone, like the first ones, where He wrote anew the words that were on the broken tablets. "And he was there with IHVH forty days and forty nights; he did neither eat bread, nor drink water. And he wrote upon the tables the words of the covenant, the ten commandments" (Ex. 34:28). When Moses came down from Sinai, with the two tablets of the Testimony, "the skin of his face shone because he had been talking with God" (Ex. 34:29).

A few remarks are self-evident when comparing the Amazonian account of recent prehistory with the biblical account of the Sinai theophanies. Firstly, as I have already pointed out, the presence in both texts of the number *three*, marking the stages in the acquisition of fire in the first case, and twice marking the "date" of the imposing Mosaic visions in the second. The space of these visions is the sacred mountain, and the time is the *third* month and the *third* day. For Kumaphari, the possession of fire finally succeeds on the *third* attempt, after his successive metamorphoses into a deer and a shrub. Let us also note that *three* wonders prove to Moses, during the first vision of Mount Horeb, that he is before the power of God: his staff is transformed into a serpent, his hand becomes leprous, and it is announced that the water of the Nile will turn into blood. Strange signs of corruption, bloodshed, and decomposition! Are they not reminiscent of the rotting body of the shaman Kumaphari, when he decides to die and let himself be devoured by birds of prey in order to steal fire from the sky?

On the other hand, while the *three* heralds the hierophanic *kairos*, the moment of the miraculous blossoming of the presence of the divine, the *four* is visibly linked to the *unification of opposites* and to what I would call the "cooking time": in other words, the four expresses the bringing together of contradictory and conflicting elements, the maturing of the *conjunctio oppositorum*, the space for reflection; the *forty* days without eating or drinking are the paradigm of this; at the end of this period, the miracle can take place, because the spirit has finally grasped the problem and the soul is ready: then God speaks, the mystery is accomplished (and here we are before the 4 + 1 or the Five as the realized and *centered* consciousness of the Four!). In the myth of the Xipaya, the Four and the Five as the center of the Four are not mentioned but, for example, the myth of the origin of fire told by the Cora Indians of Mexico, which we examined above, features a very obvious squaring of characters who, without drinking, eating, or sleeping, discuss the disappearance of fire and seek a common understanding and line of action; they find it, we recall, at the end of five days $(4 + 1 = 5)$ in the form of "illuminative" knowledge: they know that the fire is in the sky and that someone must be sent to find it.[150]

The "seventh day" raises the question of the symbolic value of Seven, but this is not the place to examine it. I will simply point out that the seventh day is the *Sabbath* when Elohim "ceased all work"; it marks the end of the creation cycle of the world. I quote our friend Armand Abécassis: "The first week thus represents the given, the raw material from which man must accomplish his task: this is what the number seven represents for the rabbis. In their language, this number is the sign of 'this world.' It is therefore entirely consistent that 'the world to come' is represented by the number eight."[151] Indeed, on Sinai, it was "on the seventh day" that IHVH called Moses to entrust him with his mission.

150　See p. 116, note 136.
151　Abécassis, *La lumière.*

IX

The Double Five and the Finger of God

Man is fire. His law, like that of all fires, is to dissolve (his envelope) and unite with the source from which he is separated.
—Louis-Claude de Saint-Martin

But the most striking feature linking the hierophany of the Burning Bush to the myth of the Xipaya Indians is the double number Five. As we have seen, the shamanic hero of the Xipaya transforms his hands into bushes, each with five branches corresponding to the five fingers of the hand. In his hand, Kumaphari receives the lit firebrand, emblematic of the sacred fire. That the brand placed in the bush by the vulture is heavenly fire becomes clear when the vulture explains how to make "domestic" fire with sticks, i.e. the mundane, utilitarian fire of cooking and heating. Kumaphari doesn't fall for the vulture's ruse; he understands very well that there are several fires, of which the one from heaven is the most precious.

This fire is celestial, of course, but also "fingerlike," as the burning bush is merely the hero's hand. Possession of the fire also appears as possession of a supra-numerary "finger," capable of communicating the magic fire without consuming itself. The combination of the two hands, five and five, thus reveals the powers of a theurgic structure whose efficacy is manifested in the acquisition of a "fire finger," which, in the myth of the Xipaya, takes the form of a lit firebrand. This structure, I repeat, when "inhabited" by celestial fire, is transformed into a 5-1-5, where the central 1 represents simultaneously, depending on the point of view, either the lit firebrand or the supra-numerary magic finger, i.e., the possession of man and the presence of Celestial Fire.

Are there any homologies between this double five and that "finger" in the biblical story? At first glance, no. But a careful reading reveals the presence of the double five in the igneous theophanies of Sinai. Indeed, we find the double five constituted by the shaman's hands in Exodus in the admittedly more subtle form of the *two* Tablets of the Law, containing the *Ten* Words of God, i.e., five Words on each Tablet. Here, fire is transformed into the divine Word. We already know that the Word is of the essence of Fire, and that this Fire burns, without consuming them, on the Tablets of stone which were written (let us emphasize) by the *finger* of IHVH. (Remember, moreover, that "tablet," or "table," comes from the Latin *tabula*, meaning "register," "table of the law," "writing tablet," etc., but also "plank of wood," "board," thus revealing the originally timbered nature of the Mosaic Tablets; for the Xipaya there are two bushes, for the Jews there are two Tablets, but they most probably have a botanic origin.) So, too, the reading from Exodus reveals a double five (and even the duplication of this double five, as the first Tablets are destroyed and God rewrites his Ten Words in two new Tablets). The central One is provided very clearly by the "finger" of IHVH, the true finger of fire. Fire thus passes from the hands of IHVH (or, more precisely, from his fingers) to the hands of Moses, who himself becomes the bearer of this Fire. This is confirmed in Exodus: "the skin of his face shone" (Ex. 34:29). So here we have a Moses of Light, comparable to the lit firebrand of the Xipaya myth, bearing Five Divine Words in each "hand": in other words, 5-1-5.

Let us try to summarize the set of homologies we have just found, which prove the archetypal nature of both the Amazonian myth and the Sinai revelations:

1   Firstly, both texts feature a hero who undergoes *three terrifying ordeals*: the three deaths of Kumaphari and the three harmful metamorphoses—the staff turned serpent, the leprous hand, and the blood-reddened water of the Nile—of which Moses is both witness and victim.

2   Then there is the presence in both cases of *a winged being* mediating celestial fire: the Angel of IHVH on Mount Horeb and the vulture in the Kumaphari legend; note, by the way, that the Portuguese phrase reported by Curt Nimuendaju and transcribed by Frazer, *gavião de anta*, means "tapir hawk" rather than "vulture," which would be *abutre*.[152]

3   In both stories, we find bushes burning with a fire that *does not consume*; for the Kumaphari myth does not say that the lit brand sets fire to the hero's fingers.[153]

4   Finally, we verify the presence, in both cases, of *a numeral structure based on the number of fingers on the hand*, i.e. two times five: on the one hand, Kumaphari's hands transformed into five-branched bushes, the support of fire from heaven; on the other, the Ten Words written by the finger of IHVH (five on each Tablet) which Moses receives (in his hands!) from the hand of God. This homology is the most surprising of all, as it reinforces the already examined idea of the archetypal nature of whole

---

152 See p. 113, note 134.

153 The flames of hell also burn without consuming, but this fire of the fallen Lucifer precludes regeneration forever. On the other hand, the fire that consumes the Phoenix (so dear to alchemists) is a regenerative fire, for it reduces the fabulous bird to ashes, but from these ashes it is reborn purified for a new life. Also, the Kundalini serpent, like a flame, ascends the tree of the spine like a fire that burns away the old man and finally transforms him into *givan mukti*, "living dead," beyond the human condition.

> numbers. It is, to say the least, astonishing (and fasci-
> nating) to see the numerical structure of the double five
> *plus* fire (Kumaphari's two hands *plus* the lit firebrand)
> reappear in the biblical story in the evolved form of the
> *Ten* Commandments written on the Two Tablets by the
> finger of IHVH.

This is certainly a powerful archetypal constellation at work in the depths of the unconscious, linked to the notion of the *Anthropos* and the co-presence in man of the divine nature. No less surprising, moreover, is the discovery of a more recent update (in the 14th century!) of the same pentagonal structure in the *Divine Comedy*, in the form of a mysterious number, "Five hundred and fifteen," to which Dante lends the immense significance of the Envoy of God! We now recognize in this number the hands of Kumaphari, the Amerindian captor of celestial fire, as well as the numerical structure of the Tablets of the Mosaic Law. But, thanks to Dante Allighieri, we also find a new "added meaning": that of the Messiah to come, the *Messo di Dio*, the Paraclete who, for Christian prophecy, will usher in the last age of mankind, that of the Fire of the Holy Spirit. A fire that I saw once again, a few days ago, in the many altars where a dove flies, of the traditional celebrations of the *Divino Paráclito*[154] of the Azores Islands, rekindled by a unanimous people who have been celebrating there, for half a millennium, the flames of Pentecost and the promised coming of the Third Person of the Holy Trinity.

---

154 Popular form of "Divine Paraclete."

www.ingramcontent.com/pod-product-compliance
Lightning Source LLC
Chambersburg PA
CBHW050003040726